the amazing cross
the central fact of history

by

SAMUEL T. CARSON

AMBASSADOR

BELFAST ◆ **GREENVILLE**
Northern Ireland ◆ South Carolina

ISBN 1 898787 44 1

AMBASSADOR PRODUCTIONS LTD,
Providence House
16 Hillview Avenue,
Belfast, BT5 6JR
Northern Ireland

Emerald House,
1 Chick Springs Road, Suite 206
Greenville,
South Carolina 29609
United States of America

contents

prologue

COUNT NIKOLAUS VON ZINZENDORF WAS THE FATHER OF MORAVIAN MISSIONS. EVEN BEFORE WILLIAM CAREY SAILED FROM HIS NATIVE ENGLAND TO CARRY THE gospel of Christ to the vast sub-continent of India, the Moravians had already established some one hundred and fifty outposts of evangelism around the world. Born in Dresden in May 1700, Zinzendorf belonged to one of the old aristocratic families of Saxony. His father died when Nikolaus was still an infant, and like Timothy, Paul's son in the faith, he owed much to the spiritual influence of both his mother and his grandmother. He traced his conversion back to a spiritual crisis in his life when he was only ten years old.

After completing a law degree at the university of Wittenberg, he went one day to Dusseldorf where an exhibition was being held in the public gallery. It was there he came to stand before Steinberg's famous painting, 'Christ on the Cross.' "It seemed", he said later, "as if the eyes of the Crucified were piercing into the depths of my soul." Then he read the inscription below the painting,

"All this I did for you;
What have you done for me?"

This proved a turning point in his life. Although the world with its fame and fortune lay at his feet, like Moses he chose to suffer affliction with the people of God, rather than to enjoy the pleasures of sin for a season. His decision had a powerful impact on the world of his day and his influence continues to the present time, "and by it he being dead, yet speaks."

He died for my sins

Some years before, while the masterpiece we have referred to was still unfinished in the artist's studio, Steinberg had a gipsy girl come and sit for him. Watching the great master at work one day, she ventured the remark, "He must have been a very wicked man to have died a death like that!" Steinberg, who was not a Christian, replied, "On the contrary, he did not die for his own sins, he died for our sins." "Did he die for your sins?" the guileless girl inquired. "Yes," said Steinberg, "He died for my sins!" But the confession was an unstudied reply to an unanticipated question and both were as arrows of conviction in his soul. Try as he would he could not shake off that conviction until in repentance and faith he sought the Saviour's grace and power.

Frances Ridley Havergal, hymnwriter and 'sweet singer of England', was competent in several languages; German, French and Italian as well as Hebrew, Greek and Latin. She also possessed poetical and musical gifts to a very high degree. Having spent some time studying in Germany she returned to that country in 1858.

This time she came accompanying her father who needed further treatment for an eye problem. Weary with her journey and glad to have finally arrived at her destination she sat down to rest. Hanging on the wall just opposite her was what seems to have been a copy of Steinberg's masterpiece. She also read the inscription. And, under the penetrating gaze of the Crucified, she too was deeply challenged as Zinzendorf had been those many years before.

A few lines spontaneously suggested themselves to her and taking a piece of paper, she jotted them down. But, dissatisfied with what she had written, she crumpled up the paper and cast it into the fire. Happily, it fell on the hearth and picking it up again she decided to keep it. Later, she was so pleased with the impression it had on her father, who was well known in his day as a writer and publisher of church music, she brought it home and eventually it found a place in many of our hymn books. To this day we are confronted with the challenge of Steinberg's painting, and of the inscription beneath it, every time we sing Miss Havergal's consecration hymn,

> *I gave My life for thee,*
> *My precious Blood I shed,*
> *That thou might'st ransomed be,*
> *And quickened from the dead.*
> *I gave My life for thee;*
> *What hast thou given for Me?*

To think of the cross simply in terms of two pieces of wood nailed over each other is to make a very great mistake. When we glory in the cross, we glory in the person of the once crucified, but now risen, Saviour. "We preach Christ crucified" was how Paul defined the preaching of the gospel. This message, when it was first preached, was foolishness to the Greeks. It's not that they poured scorn upon it, but they just could not comprehend how a man dying in weakness on a Roman stake could be, as the gospel claimed, the Saviour of all who put their trust in Him. Such philosophical and pragmatic reasoning is still a cause of stumbling to many, as it was to the Greeks all those years ago.

The Cross is Central

The startling fact is that the cross stands at the very heart of eternity. It is eternal with regard to the past, for Christ is the Lamb "who was foreordained before the foundation of the world."

(1Pet.1:20) Indeed, it might be said that there was a cross in eternity before ever there was a cross on Calvary. As for the future, the cross is also eternal, for the redeemed around the throne of God will sing the Crucified's praise and say, "Thou art worthy...for thou wast slain, and thou hast redeemed us to God by thy blood..." (Rev.5:9) And in addition to that, every calendar shows how the cross is also at the centre of history. Ages past looked forward to it, these last days are all dated from it.

Sometimes the death of Christ is spoken of as the darkest crime to have soiled the pages of the human story. This is certainly true in terms of the crucifixion; but there is another side to Calvary. And it is of paramount importance to discriminate between the two. On the one hand, *the crucifixion* is what man did to Christ, while on the other hand *the cross* is what God did in the death of His Son. It is precisely at this point the Old Testament sacrifices come to our aid. They enable us to penetrate the veil, to see beyond the darkness and to appreciate, at least to some degree, the profound and hidden mysteries of Golgotha.

While some scriptures are certainly more familiar to us than others, and some may even be more easily understood, it is never wise to say of one portion of scripture that it is more important than another. "All scripture is given by inspiration of God, and is profitable." At the same time it is unlikely that anyone will question the central place, and the vital importance, we accord to the closing chapters of the four gospels. But what is seldom realised is that those chapters find their Old Testament parallel in the opening chapters of Leviticus where we have the record of the various offerings and sacrifices of the Levitical system.

These chapters in Leviticus, when taken together, present in type, in shadow and in picture, the finer details and the deeper mysteries of that amazing work of atonement, the accomplishment of which is detailed with such care in the closing chapters of the gospels. Both sets of chapters stand related to each other as type is related to antitype.

Where shall we begin?

Of the five principle offerings in the Levitical system, the first was the Burnt Offering. Its most notable feature was, that *in its totality* it was placed on the altar; it was all for God. Whereas in the other offerings, the sacrifice was divided, and part was laid on the altar, and part given to the priest or to the offerer. The Burnt Offering therefore, speaks of total consecration to the will of God; first Christ's consecration, and then ours.

This one offering, sometimes called 'the whole burnt offering', invests the cross with a meaning so sublime, it should cause our whole beings to be bowed in reverent worship. Here, almost every other consideration is set aside, so that one supreme purpose might be realised: above everything else, the Father's will must be done and the Father's name must be glorified. The glory of God was intrinsic in the work of the cross.

The final offering of the five was the Trespass Offering. It deals with the matter of our sins, it points to "Christ, who was delivered for our offences." (Rom.4:25) When viewed from the standpoint of the Christian's experience, this offering comes first, because the first step in becoming a Christian is to recognise that we are sinners, guilty before God, and in danger of judgement.

When we first learned our need, the cry went up, "What must I do to be saved?" The gospel answer was to point us to Christ, our great Trespass Offering, who died for our sins according to the scriptures. And the gospel message was, "Believe on the Lord Jesus Christ, and you will be saved." (Acts 16:31) This precise message was first addressed by Paul to the gaoler at Phillipi and it is just the same for us to-day.

And so we may look at these five offerings in two ways. If it is a question of how God has been glorified in the cross, then we must begin with the Burnt Offering. On the other hand, if it is a question of how we may become right with God, then we must begin with the Trespass Offering. Our purpose in this study is to take the offerings in the order in which they are given.

We shall begin, therefore, with the Burnt Offering and learn that the cross, in its most intense character, was something that was accomplished in the first instance for the glory of God. And then, working our way through the other offerings we shall come to the Trespass Offering, and discover how the cross, besides glorifying God, is the instrument by which God is able to comprehensively meet the deepest need of the human heart and conscience.

> *In the cross of Christ I glory,*
> *Towering o'er the wrecks of time;*
> *All the light of sacred story,*
> *Gathers round its head sublime.*

preface

THE BIBLE BEGINS WITH THE FIVE BOOKS OF MOSES,
COMMONLY REFERRED TO AS THE PENTATEUCH. THE
CENTRAL BOOK OF THE FIVE IS THE BOOK OF LEVITICUS.
This book begins with the God of Sinai, speaking to Moses,
not from the mount that burned with fire, but from within the
veil, from off the mercy-seat which was stained with the blood
of sacrifice. The voice Moses heard was not one of terror or of
judgement, it was a voice of wondrous grace. God was in the
midst of His people. His dwelling place was the Tabernacle,
the completion and erection of which is described in the final
chapter of Exodus.

This fact gives a special character to the book of Leviticus,
which we rightly call the book of the sanctuary. Everything in
this book is viewed from the standpoint of the sanctuary of God.
Its opening chapters detail the various offerings and sacrifices
upon which the religious life of the nation was established.
Moreover, everything in these chapters pointed forward to, and
found it's fulfilment in, the one great sacrifice of Calvary. The
Levitical offerings were not special because of any intrinsic value
in them, but because each one of them set forth some distinct
aspect of the work of the cross and of the person of our Lord
Jesus Christ.

The Types

From the garden of Eden, the sacrifice of Calvary, which is the central fact of history, was foreshadowed through object lessons of one kind or another. It was prefigured across the ages by many remarkable persons and unusual events. And then, as the reality and substance drew near, the shadows became more and more clearly defined. These various object lessons, which we may in broad terms, call pictures or types, serve to clothe in material form the great principles and doctrines which gather around the cross of Christ.

Strictly speaking, types are different from figures of speech which abound in every language. They are also to be distinguished from what is merely allegorical or simply illustrative. The types themselves embodied spiritual truth to the people of the time when they were first given. And so when a person, event or ceremonial used in the Old Testament finds its parallel in New Testament truth we call this a type. Christ Himself is the superlative antitype since the one subject of both parts of scripture is the testimony of Jesus. The historical meaning of the type should first be dilligently established for only then are we in a position to identify the truth which it foreshadows.

The Old Testament books in general, and the five books of Moses in particular, abound in types which, as a rule, find their antitype or fulfilment in the New Testament. But there are exceptions to this rule. For instance, Joseph is universally seen as a type of Christ, and yet nowhere in the New Testament is he specifically recognised as such. Because of this some prefer to read the story of Joseph in an allegorical rather than in a typical way. Again, Paul referred to Israel's wilderness history, and without being very specific, claims that *all these things* happened unto them for examples or types. (See 1Cor.10:11.)

To understand and appreciate the types it is necessary to cultivate a spiritual mind, a mind that can receive impressions from the Holy Spirit, impressions which in turn, are capable of being tested by the scriptures themselves. The types of the Old Testament have been described as the very alphabet or language in which the New Testament was written. It follows that to dogmatically refuse the types must be as unreasonable as it would be to assert that *'this* is *that'* of every detail without having some definite scripture warrant for doing so.

To say that Satan has scored a great tactical victory over the Christian church in this area is simply to state the obvious. For all practical purposes the pulpits have fallen silent on the typical scriptures and to many believers they are virtually a closed book. True, some have carried these things beyond reasonable measure, while others have attempted to build their doctrines on the types, instead of on the New Testament. But failure in others is no excuse for us to be intimidated into such gross neglect. The net result is the very great impoverishment of the church of God.

We emphasise that it is always necessary when reading the scriptures, to insist that we do not take our doctrine from the types. But discovering the doctrine in the New Testament, we then turn to the types, and find marvellous and God given illustrations which elucidate and make plain the doctrine we have already received. The typical scriptures are like windows in a house, they let the light shine through. They present in pictorial form the truth we are otherwise so slow to apprehend. They also enable us to distinguish the finer points of doctrine which otherwise might be an occasion of division among us.

Our warrant for exploring these things is found in the New Testament where we are quite clearly taught that, "The things which were written aforetime were written for our learning, that we, through patience and comfort of the scriptures, might have hope." (Rom.15:4. See also Luke 24:25-27, 44-46.) When taken together, the five offerings, detailed in the first seven chapters of Leviticus, give us a multi-dimensional picture of the person and work of our Saviour, the Lord Jesus Christ. The offerings combine to present an amazing insight into God's thoughts concerning His Son. They show us, from one angle and then another, the sorrows and death of the cross.

All the instruction contained in the book of Leviticus must have been given to Moses during the period between the completion of the Tabernacle in the plains of Sinai, and the signal to resume the journey towards Caanan, which was given forty five days later. An important detail to be borne in mind in this connection is that, although the offerings are recorded first (chapters 1-7), the consecration of the priests (chapters 8-10) must, of necessity, have come before the inauguration of the sacrificial system. The significance of this order should not be overlooked.

A Divine Order

God is a God of order, and this is seen in the order in which these things are presented. The very order itself is a reminder to us that Calvary is the basis of everything in God's plan. Not only of our salvation, but of our service as well. In the spiritual realm, only what is related to, and grounded in, the work of Christ upon the cross is finally significant. And the offerings are recorded first to teach us also that Calvary must be the inspiration of all that we do. Only when this is true in our own experience can we say with any degree of sincerity, "The love of Christ constrains us." (2Cor.5:14)

The pre-eminent message of the book of Leviticus is that all true worship and service finds its impulse in the one great sacrifice of the Cross. The Jewish sacrifices pointed forward to this and, on the basis of those sacrifices, the Israelites themselves were constituted the worshipping people of God.

As already noted in the *prologue*, the precise order in which the sacrifices are presented is significant. It reflects the new situation between God and man as a result of sin. God is holy but we are unholy, by nature we are sinners lost and ruined. When first convicted of our lost estate and led to Christ in repentance and faith, the question of our trespasses was paramount in our minds. Nothing else mattered, just the question of our sins. And yet, the record of the Sin Offering and of the Trespass Offering is placed last of all.

But then, as we began to grow in grace and in the knowledge of Christ, we gradually came to realise that there is more to our redemption than simply the forgiveness of sins. God's holiness had to be satisfied, and a ground of reconciliation established which would enable man to enjoy peace with God. This required a sacrifice, like the Peace Offering, a sacrifice which none but Jesus Christ could offer.

But even when we understood that, the greatest discovery of all was yet to be made. We gradually came to see that in the cross our Saviour's devotion to the will of His Father reached its high water mark. He came out from heaven declaring, "I come to do your will, O my God." (Psa.40:7,8) And as He went to the cross He was heard to say, "Not my will, but yours be done." In that once for all work of atonement accomplished on earth, there was something that absorbed the interest of heaven. Simply stated, this is the essential message of the Burnt Offering.

How much did they know?

It is always difficult to judge how much Moses and Aaron were able to enter into the meaning of the system of offerings they had established. They had the word of the Lord, and we cannot but admire their ready obedience to it. And while many and varied moral and spiritual lessons may be drawn from the lives of those two outstanding Old Testament characters, we have an advantage over them. We live on the resurrection side of the sacrifice their offerings portrayed.

Moreover, in the scriptures of the New Testament, the Holy Spirit has placed in our hands the wonderful key that unlocks the treasures of the Levitical system which, in turn, reveals to us the secrets of the Father's heart and the deep mysteries of the Saviour's cross and passion. Unbelief may dismiss these things as far-fetched and even mystical. But to the renewed mind and the regenerate heart, they are reality indeed.

A young woman was given a novel to read, but finding it dry and uninteresting she tossed it aside and forgot it. Presently, she fell in love with a young man who, as it happened, was the author of that novel. She searched it out again, and found it the most fascinating book she had ever read. The moral is quite clear: to appreciate some things requires us to have a certain attitude of heart and mind. This is certainly true in reading the scriptures in general and the offerings in particular. May the Lord grant us help and blessing as we apply ourselves to these things.

the burnt offering

(Scripture Leviticus 1:1-17, 6:8-13)

N.T. Fulfilment - "Christ has given Himself for us an offering and a sacrifice to God for a sweet smelling savor." Ephesians 5:2

THE BURNT OFFERING WAS THE FIRST OF THE FIVE PRINCIPAL OFFERINGS IN THE LEVITICAL SYSTEM, AND THE WAY WAS ALWAYS OPEN FOR AN ISRAELITE TO BRING a Burnt Offering. The primary idea behind this offering was acceptance with God, acceptance on the basis of accomplished atonement. The phrase, "he shall offer it of his own volountary will" (v.3), is better rendered, 'he shall offer it for his acceptance'.

In some tribal lands even to this day a person seeking an audience with the Chief would first send a present. If his present is accepted, he is assured that all is well. If not, then discretion being the better part of valour, it is wise for him to withdraw as quietly as possible.

At the gates of Eden, Cain and Abel presented their respective offerings to the Lord. Only Abel's offering was accepted and God accepted Abel's person in accepting his offering. "By faith Abel offered unto God a more excellent sacrifice than Cain, by which he obtained witness that he was righteous, God testifying of his gifts: and by it he being dead yet speaks." (Hebs.11:4) The Burnt Offering speaks of Christ's acceptance, and while sin may be implied, it is not the primary thought, the immediate idea is Christ's own acceptance before God and the consequent acceptance in Him of all who belong to Him.

Bringing a Burnt Offering was an act of pure worship. When Noah came out of the ark he built an altar and offered burnt offerings, and since this is the first direct reference in scripture to the burnt offering, it beautifully illustrates its meaning. It was an expression of worship on the part of a saved man. (See Gen.8:20.)

Man was created in the image of God and for God, and his chief end is to glorify God. The old commandment said, "You shall worship the Lord your God and Him only shall you serve". (Matt.4:10) The reality is, however, that all of us stand accused of the charge laid against Belshazzar, the last king of Babylon, "The God in whose hand your breath is, and whose are all your ways, have you not glorified." (Dan.5:23)

But the man Christ Jesus stands apart as the one grand exception to this rule. His holy life vindicated God's name in a world in which it had been dishonoured, and by His perfect obedience, even unto death, the outraged righteousness of God was entirely satisfied and God was glorified. In proof of this, Jesus was brought again from the dead, and exalted to the Father's right hand. And now, because of His acceptance in Heaven, the acceptance of all who are in Him is assured.

Acceptance in Christ

If, under the Levitical system someone brought to the door of the Tabernacle an offering for his acceptance, he first identified himself with the offering by laying his hand on the victim's head. Then, after it was slain, the offering was burned on the brazen altar. All this was done because God had promised, "it shall be accepted for him to make atonement for him." (Lev.1:4)

Note, it is not '*he* shall be accepted' but rather '*it* shall be accepted." The emphasis is upon the acceptance of the offering, as the ground of the offerers own acceptance. Moreover, the tense of the verb does not look to the distant future, it denotes immediate acceptance and certain assurance. The offerer would know, there and then, that he was divinely accepted because his offering had been received.

There was also a laying on of hands by the offerer in the case of the Sin Offering, and these two present the two sides of imputation. In the latter case, there was a ceremonial transference of the sins of the offerer to the sacrifice. But in the case of the Burnt Offering, the laying on of hands signified a transference of the merit and value of the sacrifice to the offerer.

To see the Lord Jesus in the Burnt Offering does not require exceptional spiritual insight. The parallels are clearly drawn. Of ourselves we have nothing to commend us to God; but there is one who is worthy, and identifying ourselves with Him by faith we become 'in Christ'. And being 'in Him' we find acceptance before God. "We are accepted in the Beloved." (Eph.1:6) Its not just that our deficiency is supplied by His sufficiency, we are actually placed 'in Christ'. And God has given us blessed assurance of these things in that He has raised His Son from the dead.

Of course, as already stated, all is on the basis of accomplished atonement. And while this is not the principle thought in the Burnt Offering, nevertheless the sin question must be settled. The cross, as seen in the Offerings, lays to rest any query that might ever be raised about God's attitude to sin, on the one hand, or to holiness on the other. We shall see this matter brought out with emphasis in other offerings, but, for the present, we again insist that the primary idea in the Burnt Offering is the matter of our acceptance before God.

Some look upon the cross simply as the place where sin found its full and final answer, and where the great adversary was vanquished. Now the cross was all that, but it was much more. Calvary was the place where Christ's love for the Father was fully displayed, and where God, in every attribute of His being was glorified. And here in the Burnt Offering we are able to see how the Lord Jesus went to Calvary because of His delight in the Father's will. "The cup that my Father gives me shall I not drink it?" To see Him as the sin-bearer settles the conscience, but to see Him doing the Father's will, even unto death, wins and warms the heart, in a peculiar way this engages the affections. Hence, there is brought before us in this offering, an aspect of the cross that can only be ultimately comprehended by the mind of God.

Significant Details

With this basic thought established we can now look at some of the details of the Burnt Offering. Every facet of it points to Him in whom our faith has found a resting place. The offering was presented at the door of the Tabernacle before the brazen altar. Any one of five sacrifices could have been chosen for a Burnt Offering. Besides reflecting the ability or otherwise of the offerer, this variety of sacrifice may also anticipate the many different facets of Christ's wonderful person. They may speak of the many and variegated features that enter into what are termed 'the unsearchable riches of Christ'.

If, for instance, the offering was a bullock it was slain at the gate before the altar, and its blood was sprinkled round about the altar v.5. This meant that all who approached, from north, south, east or west, did so on ground sprinkled with the blood of sacrifice. The spiritual mind will readily perceive the significance of this. There is only one ground upon which we can approach God. That is the ground of Jesus' blood.

Moreover it is important to see that by the shedding of His blood our Saviour not only made atonement for sin, and established a basis for sinners to find acceptance before God: He also opened up a way of access, so that we can approach God's throne of grace as believer-priests. The sacrificial work of Christ allows us now to claim, "boldness to enter into the holiest by the blood of Jesus." (Hebs.10:19)

> *We stand upon His merit,*
> *We know no other stand;*
> *Not e'en where glory dwelleth,*
> *In Immanuel's land.*

Looking 'into' Jesus

After this the Burnt Offering was flayed and cut into its pieces. v.6. This exercise has an important parallel for us. Our appreciation of Christ will not amount to very much if we are content to dwell on vague generalisations about His person and His work. We must look into every aspect of His wonderful life, we must view our unique Saviour from every conceivable standpoint. When hidden treasure is uncovered by some archeological expedition, then the experts come along and carefully itemise the various pieces found. We need to itemise the various aspects of the person and work of our Lord Jesus Christ and we need to study them one by one.

We should think deeply of Christ 'before time', as well as of Christ 'in time'. We should ponder Him in His life on earth, viewing Him at Nazareth, at Galilee and at Jerusalem. And we should dwell much upon His death of shame. We should reflect often on His present ministry as the Great High Priest of His people. And we should maintain a constant watching for His return, when He will come to receive from the world His own. This is what it means for us to flay the Burnt Offering and to cut it into its pieces. In the event, the more we get to know Him, the more we learn to love Him and the more our confidence in Him increases.

All on the Altar

The priest was then responsible for taking the pieces and burning 'all on the altar' (v.9). The word used of the Sin Offering which was burned without the camp, means 'to consume in anger'. It speaks of the Lord Jesus Christ who suffered without the gate. The fire of God's wrath fell on Him when He was made sin for us. But the word used here is different, it means to 'eat up with delight'. It suggests a slow burning, like the burning of incense, so that it leaves a fragrance lingering in the air. Jesus could say, "the zeal of thine house has eaten me up." Hence we are able to identify the New Testament answer to the Burnt Offering in what Paul wrote to the Ephesians, "Christ has given Himself for us an offering and a sacrifice to God for a sweet smelling savour." (Eph.5:2)

This verse also explains why the Burnt Offering is called the Whole Burnt Offering, and why we speak of it as the offering of consecration. In the other offerings there was a part for man and a part for God, but in this all was for God. Except for the skin, it was laid in its entirety on the altar of sacrifice. The skin was not burned; it remained as proof that a sacrifice had actually taken place. The skin, given to the officiating priest, might also call to mind the coats of skin with which God covered the nakedness of our first parents in the garden of Eden.

It may be beyond our comprehension, but it is wondrously true, that when God gave Christ, He gave His all. This must have been so, because "all the fullness of the Godhead bodily dwells in Him." (Col. 2:9) What more could God have given than when "He so loved the world that He gave His only begotten Son?" (John 3:16) Paul witnessed to the totality of God's giving: "He that spared not His own Son, but delivered Him up for us all, how shall He not with Him freely give us all things" (Rom.8:32).

> *O blessed God, what hast thou done!*
> *How vast a ransom paid!*
> *Who could conceive God's only Son*
> *Upon the altar laid?*

At the same time we must recognise that Christ gave His all when He gave Himself. What more could He have given than

to give Himself? The Burnt Offering signifies Christ's entire sur-
render to the Father's will: He held nothing back. To give oneself
is total commitment, and "Christ loved the church, and gave
Himself for it." (Eph.5:25) Again, "the Son of God, loved me and
gave Himself for me." (Gal.2:20) Pause and reflect on those three
words, 'Himself for me.' What a phenomenal exchange, what a
tremendous substitution.

> *I stand amazed in the presence,*
> *Of Jesus the Nazarene;*
> *And wonder how He could love me,*
> *A sinner condemned, unclean.*

What shall I render ?

But the consecration that is seen in the Burnt Offering, also
raises the question of our committment to the Lord. "What shall
I render unto the Lord for all His benefits"? Shall I give more, or
shall I give less, or shall I give all to Him? The communion service is primarily a memorial feast, when we reflect on what God
has done for us in giving His Son; and on what Christ has done
in giving Himself. But it is surely more than that.

The Lord's supper is an occasion when we affirm afresh
our love and loyalty to Him who so loved us. There must be an
inadequacy about our eating the bread and drinking the wine, if
that act is simply a memorial and not at the same time the token
of an inward consecration; the outward sign and seal that our all
has been laid upon the altar of sacrifice.

Besides being taken from the herd or the flock, the Burnt
Offering may have been taken from the fowl, in which case it
was an offering of turtledoves or young pigeons. (Lev.1:14) As
already noted, a bullock, a lamb or a pigeon would probably have
reflected the ability of the offerer. A rich man could bring a bullock whereas a poor man might only be able to bring a pigeon.

When our Lord was presented in the Temple by Mary and
Joseph on the eighth day, the offering was a poor man's offering.

(See Luke 2:21-24.) Could there have been a more eloquent witness to the truth so clearly stated by Paul, "you know the grace of our Lord Jesus Christ, that, though He was rich, yet for your sakes He became poor, that you through His poverty might be rich." (2Cor.8:9)?

The poor man's offering

When a bird was presented as a Burnt Offering, detailed instructions were given to the priest about how it was to be handled. And taken together those several instructions looked forward, in a most profound way, to 'the death of the cross'. Since it is now given to us to view things from the resurrection side of Calvary we cannot but be deeply impressed by the amazing correspondence between the type and its fulfilment.

(1) Violent

The bird foreshadowed the death of Christ as *a violent death*. The priest would take the bird and, *'wring off its head'* and then the blood would be, *'wrung out at the side of the altar'* (v.15). Even in the reading of these words we can almost feel the violence. What a remarkable anticipation of the ill-treatment, the buffeting and the violence meted out to Him who "had done no violence, neither was any deceit in His mouth." (Isa.53:9) We can never forget the pain that He suffered and how they spat in His face and plucked the hairs from His cheeks.

Nor can we forget that, before He was crucified, He was handed over to the soldiers to be scourged. This involved the victim being spreadeagled on a frame and then beaten with the Roman lash. It was accepted that forty strokes would kill a man, so they gave Him thirty-nine. After that they led Him away, bearing His cross, to Golgotha, the place of a skull. And down through the centuries to this very day we still seem to hear,

> " ... the dull blow
> of the hammer swung low,
> they are nailing the Lord to the tree."

Then there was the piercing of His hands and of His feet. (Psa.22:16) There was also the crown of thorns pressed upon His brow, and the spear thrust into His side. All this and much more entered into Peter's telling phrase, "He...by wicked hands...was crucified and slain." (Acts 2:23)

(2) Humiliating

The death of Christ would also be *a humiliating death*. The priest would take the bird of the burnt offering and "pluck away its crop with its feathers, and cast it...by the place of the ashes" (v.16). All the glory of the bird was to be cast in the dust and esteemed as nothing at all. It is a most solemn thing for God to humble a man. He humbled the king of Babylon, so that his reason left him, and for seven years he ate grass like the wild beasts. A better way is for man to humble himself. "Humble yourselves under the mighty hand of God." In this, our supreme example is Christ. "He humbled Himself and became obedient unto death, even the death of the cross." (Phil.2:8)

There was much more to the dark side of Calvary than the pain, for in addition to that there was the shame. In the hour of His death our dear Saviour was also humiliated. He was set forth naked upon a Roman stake, He became the song of the drunkards and a public spectacle before all who passed by,

'Lord, we can ne'er forget the shame ...'

Nor can we forget that besides being rejected of men He was also despised. (Isa.53:3) This is the word the prophet Daniel used to describe Antiochus Epiphanes, whose name remains to this day, the most infamous in all the many annals of Jewish history. (Dan.11:21) We should regularly take time to reflect and to "Consider Him that endured such contradiction of sinners against Himself. (Hebs.12:3)

Bearing shame and scoffing rude,
In my place condemned He stood;
Sealed my pardon with His blood:
Hallelujah! what a Saviour.

25

At this point it is necessary to distinguish again between 'the death of the cross' and 'the crucifixion'. The former was the supreme expression of God's saving grace, while the latter was the greatest crime ever perpetrated in the long and lamentable history of human evil. Although enacted simultaneously, they stand apart from each other in character, as far as the east is from the west. What we have said so far has been mainly on the side of our Saviour's crucifixion; but the bird of the burnt offering brings before us the other side of Calvary as well.

(3) Mysterious

The death of Christ would also be *a mysterious death.* There was a limit to what man could do and a point beyond which he could not go. This was foreshadowed in a restriction placed on the priest in his handling of the bird of the Burnt Offering. "He shall cleave it with the wings thereof, but shall not divide it asunder" (v.17). If the limitation is applied to the cross in a purely physical sense, it might refer to the fact that having broken the legs of the two who were crucified with Him, the soldiers did not break the legs of our Saviour, for they saw that He was dead already. This of course was done that the scripture might be fulfilled, "A bone of Him shall not be broken."

What God did

But the meaning of the limitation is surely deeper than that. Not all the shame men heaped upon Him, nor all the things He suffered at the hands of the wicked, could atone for human sin. Beyond question, the crucifixion of the Son of God was the high water mark of human guilt. But when man had done his worst, God stepped in and veiled that terrible scene from human view. The sun withheld its shining and Calvary became shrouded in a supernatural darkness. It was then that God did what only God could do, "He made Him, who knew no sin, to be sin for us, that we might be made the righteousness of God in Him." (2Cor.5:21) Moreover, what God did in the death of Christ was fully done, and it will never need to be done again.

It is true that our Lord was rejected by the Jews and crucified by the Romans. But beyond all that they combined to do, it stands revealed that "God was in Christ, reconciling the world unto Himself." (2Cor.5:19) The death and resurrection of Christ are two parts of one divine whole. Just as man had no part in His resurrection, he could have had no part in the atonement that was accomplished through His death.

(4) Voluntary

Reference is also made to the wings of the Burnt Offering bird. "He shall cleave it with the wings thereof" (v.17). Two hundred years ago Samuel Stennett wrote,

> *He left His starry crown,*
> *And laid His robes aside,*
> *On wings of love came down,*
> *And wept, and bled, and died:*
> *What He endured no tongue can tell,*
> *To save our souls from death and hell.*

This seems to catch the significance of the wings. The death of Christ would be *a voluntary death*. None of the things done to the Burnt Offering bird could have been done unless that bird had first come down from heaven to earth. Time and again the enemies of our Lord would have laid their hands upon Him but His hour was not yet come. But when the hour came, when God's clock struck, He voluntarily subjected Himself to all the indignities that were heaped upon Him. The voluntary nature of what He did is emphasised by the repetition of the emphatic pronoun, He "made *Himself* of no reputation...He humbled *Himself* and became obedient unto death, even the death of the cross." (Phil.2:7,8)

But Paul goes on, "Wherefore, God also has highly exalted Him..." (Phil.2:9) The 'wherefore' seems to teach that Christ's present exaltation, is to be seen as a reward for His self-humbling. It is the receipt and the ultimate proof that His sacrifice has been accepted in heaven. He is there, and in His acceptance we are able to read the measure of our own. This is the essential message of the Burnt Offering. It tells of an accepted sacrifice, and it proclaims the believer's acceptance on the basis of an accomplished atonement.

The last word about the Burnt Offering in Leviticus chapter one is that it was "a sweet savour unto the Lord". Not all the offerings were of a sweet savour, the exceptions were the sin and trespass offerings. (Although that part of the sin offering which was burned on the altar was said to have been a sweet savour unto the Lord.) God demanded a sin offering and God demanded a trespass offering, but the Burnt Offering was not a matter of demand. As already noted, the Burnt Offering was an act of pure worship, it was the volountary expression of the offerer's devotion to the Lord. He offered it "of his own voluntary will" (v3). It was constrained by love rather than by law.

Love was the motivation that lay behind the self-humbling of the Lord of glory. "The Son of God loved me and gave Himself for me." (Gal.2:20) And again, "Christ loved us, and gave Himself for us an offering and a sacrifice to God for a sweet smelling savour." (Eph.5:2) And "Christ also loved the Church, and gave Himself for it." (Eph.5:25)

> *Oh 'twas love, 'twas wondrous love,*
> *The love of God to me;*
> *It brought my Saviour from above,*
> *To die on Calvary.*

His Love and Ours

But if the Burnt Offering speaks of Christ and His great love for us, it also speaks of our love for Him. These two are cause and consequence. "We love Him, because He first loved us." (1John 4:19) The Psalmist used only twelve letters to write the bottom line of godly testimony through the ages, "I love the

Lord." (Psa.116:1) At the communion table the Lord still enquires of His own "lovest thou me"? Our fitness to be there can be measured by the degree in which we are able to reply, "Yea Lord, thou knowest that I love thee." (John 21:15-17)

Reference has been made to the fact that the ability of the offerer was taken into account in bringing a Burnt Offering. A wealthier man might bring a bullock from the herd, a poorer man might bring a lamb from the flock. One requirement however was common to all; the offering had to be without blemish. An inferior gift will not do for God.

Love gives its best

Nor will true love be satisfied to give less than its very best. The Christians at Ephesus had "left their first love". (Rev.2:4) The word here translated *first* is elsewhere translated *best*. (See Luke 15:22.) It would seem that whereas there was a time when nothing but the best would have done for God, these Ephesian Christians were now prepared to offer God something less than their very best. Here is a simple rule of thumb by which we can test our love for the Lord, are we giving to God just our second best, or at any rate, something less than our very best?

The other side of the equation is that real love will never ask for more. According to human estimation the poor man's offering may come a long way short of what another man brought, but in God's sight it was of equal value. The great principle is that with God it is accepted according to what a man has and not according to what he has not. The two mites cast into the treasury by the widow were more precious to the Lord than the far larger amounts given by those who merely gave out of their abundance. The widow alone had given her all.

It should be noted that the two mites allowed her a choice. Only one mite would have required that she give all or nothing; two mites meant that she could have retained a half and given a half. The widow's devotion was seen in that she gave her all. Our Lord asks of us our very best. Shall we who profess to love Him, be satisfied to offer Him anything less?

> *Naught that I have, mine own I'll call,*
> *I'll hold it for the giver.*
> *My Lord, my life, my way, my all*
> *Are His and His forever.*

the meal offering

(Scripture Leviticus 2:1-16, 6:14-18.)

N.T. Fulfilment - "Who did no sin, neither was guile found in His mouth . . . who His own self bore our sins in His own body on the tree." (1Pet.2:22-24)

FOLLOWING THE BURNT OFFERING WHERE THE CHIEF EMPHASIS WAS UPON OUR ACCEPTANCE BEFORE GOD, WE COME NOW TO CONSIDER THE MEAL OFFERING and here our attention is focussed on that wonderful person by whom our acceptance has been secured. We are here permitted to trace the character of the life He lived as a man among men, which He yielded up voluntarily to death, even the death of the cross, and then took again, but now in resurrection power. Here we are also able to glimpse the life that He now lives, for He lives in the power of an endless life.

A life laid down

The Meal or cereal (*a.v.* meat) Offering, sometimes referred to as the gift offering because of its association with the harvest, was distinguished from all the other offerings by the absence of the shedding of blood. Unlike the other offerings, the Meal Offering speaks primarily of the life that our Saviour laid down in death rather than of the death itself. It is a well attested fact that the death Jesus died took its character from the life He lived. Had the Crucified not been who and what He was, His death could not have had the significance with which scripture invests it. The Meal Offering is a heaven drawn picture of Christ's perfect life.

Among those born of women, Jesus Christ stands alone, and unique without peer, equal or rival. Many devout minds have attempted to define and circumscribe the history of Christ, whose pilgrimage on earth extended to just thirty three years. The study usually divides into two parts, the first part relating to His Person and to all that entered into His life among men, and the second taking up the great issues raised by His death and resurrection. But the mind of man can never comprehend the immeasurable dimensions of either His Person or His Work.

The difficulties become immediately evident when it is claimed that the Word who became flesh and dwelt among us "was in the beginning with God." (John 1:1,14) Or how can we understand a man who lived some two thousand years after Abraham had lived and died, and yet claimed to have been before Abraham? If He is God, how could He be born of a woman and die on a cross? If He is merely man, how could He have authority to forgive sins, or to speak to the winds and the waves in such a way that compelled them to obey Him? The answer to all these questions and countless others lies in the fact, that He is God *and* man in one unique and incomparable person.

Under Attack

Times without number the Christian church has had to set itself for the defence of the gospel. Through the years every aspect of truth has come under attack; but most often the prime target has been the Person of Christ. Sometimes the aim has been to undermine belief in His deity, while at other times the attack has concentrated on His humanity. The Arian controversy in the fourth century was an attempt, probably deeper and darker than any other, to undermine the faith. Arius denied the deity of Christ, arguing that He was inferior to the Father, although the first and noblest of all the created beings God the Father had made out of nothing. The controversy spread throughout the world disturbing the outward peace of the church and dividing the entire Christian profession.

But His real and perfect humanity has also come under powerful attack. In the long story of the human race the Lord Jesus Christ was the only perfect man to appear on the stage of history. Every virtue met in Him. He was perfect in thought, in word and in action. Although subjected to the most intense scrutiny by both earth and heaven, in the end, He could silence His accusers with the challenge, "Which of you convinces me of sin?" The Meal Offering has in view the amazing uniqueness of Christ who laid down a perfect life, when He "gave Himself for us an offering and a sacrifice to God." (Eph. 5:2)

The great divide

The cross has rightly been spoken of as the great divide. It divides time and it divides eternity. It also divides humanity for it is by our attitude to the cross that we demonstrate whose we are, and whom we serve. During the Roman period hundreds of people died by crucifixion, but none of those deaths had such profound and far reaching effects as have sprung from the death of Christ. This is because of who He is; and because of the perfection of His Person.

Jesus Christ is "God manifest in flesh." (1Tim.3:16) And because of this, the death of Christ has ramifications that extend to the limits of the universe itself. It has accomplished eternal redemption for us, and it will yet be the cause of everlasting righteousness being established in our world, a world where sin has been allowed to demonstrate its utter sinfulness.

What think you of Christ? is still the test, that tries both our faith and our creed. Because there is presently such a feeble apprehension of the person of Christ, many are being side-tracked into a multitude of erroneous systems. They need to be alerted to the plain, unvarnished fact that to be wrong on the person of Christ means that we are wrong all along the line. Recovery from some of these systems can be a very painful business. It is better to refuse them out of hand, particularly when we find them false regarding some aspect of our Lord's glorious person.

Fine Flour

The basic ingredient of the Meal Offering was the fine flour. This speaks of the perfect manhood of our Saviour. Flour, corn and bread are regularly used in scripture to set forth Christ as the food of His people. Jesus said, "I am the bread of life." And alluding to the manna that came down from heaven and lay upon the face of the wilderness, He said, "I am the living bread that came down from heaven." (John 6:51)

The fineness of the flour is significant. It was flour without lumps or irregularities. Such was the texture of the flour, it would pass easily through a sieve. We are not like that; we are liable to be coarse and ill-tempered, especially under provocation. At our best moments there is little evenness with us, one grace is sure to predominate at the expense of another. With Him all was in perfect balance. We require a great deal of milling, grinding and crushing to refine us and to mould us in some small measure after His image.

But our Lord, even under the most intense provocation was like fine flour. "When He was reviled, He reviled not again; when He suffered, He threatened not, but committed Himself to Him who judges righteously." (1Pet.2:23) In the Lord Jesus every grace blended in perfect harmony and balance. God's law laid down that everything offered in sacrifice should be perfect. "It shall be perfect to be accepted." (Lev.22:21) And this was uniquely true of our Lord from the cradle to the grave. The things He suffered did not create the fine flour character, they simply served to draw it forth and to reveal it. Not only did earth and heaven bear witness to this, but even hell itself contributed its own unsolicited witness to the impeccable life of the man Christ Jesus.

The Oil of the Spirit

Throughout scripture, oil is a constantly recurring emblem or type of the Holy Spirit, and oil is very prominent in the offering before us. The Meal Offering may have had oil poured upon it, or it may have been mingled with oil, or it may have been anointed with oil. (See Lev.2:1,4.) These references seem to anticipate the unique relationship that existed between the Holy Spirit and the man Christ Jesus throughout His life and ministry in this world.

The pouring of the oil on the Meal Offering may refer to the fact that the Holy Spirit in all the plenitude of His power always rested upon Christ. (See Isa.11:2.) "God gave not the Spirit by measure unto Him." (John 3:34) That He was conceived of the Holy Ghost and born of the virgin Mary may be the thought behind the Meal offering being mingled with oil. Matthew's simple yet profound testimony is that Mary "was found with child of the Holy Spirit." (Matt. 1:18)

The anointing with oil seems to relate to His baptism. The Holy Spirit in the form of a dove descended and abode upon Him. All the evangelists record the baptism and agree that it signalled the induction to His public ministry. Shortly after His baptism He stood in the synagogue at Nazareth and said, "the Spirit of the Lord is upon me, He has anointed me to preach the gospel to the poor." (Luke 4:18.) Throughout the entire course of that ministry He was 'led by the Spirit'. 'He returned in the power of the Spirit,' and He always walked in the consciousness of the Spirit's fullness resting upon Him.

Preparing the Meal Offering

Three ways of preparing the Meal Offering are identified. It may have been baked (1) in an oven, (2) on an open pan or griddle, or (3) in the frying pan. (Lev.2:4-7) It would not be wise to dogmatise on the spiritual significance of these things. But having in mind that 'all scripture is given by inspiration of God, and is profitable,' we must consider them to be meaningful.

If righteous Lot was vexed with the filthy conversation of the wicked in Sodom, what must have been the vexations of the sinless Son of God as He passed through this sin-soaked world? How often He must have 'groaned within Himself.' Mark tells us in one chapter how He looked up to heaven and sighed, and then in the next chapter that He sighed deeply in His spirit. Many of the messianic psalms tell of the inward groanings of our Lord both in life and in death. These things may answer to the Meal Offering baked in the oven, for what goes on in the oven is concealed from view.

The open pan or griddle might refer to the sufferings He endured at the hands of wicked men. Put to an open shame, He was made a public spectacle in the presence of all who passed by. Similarly, the frying pan might refer to what He endured in those hours of darkness when He became sin for us. In contrast to the oven and even the griddle, what is prepared in the frying pan takes only a short time. It was in just three hours on dark Calvary that all the waves and billows of God's wrath fell upon Jesus as God laid on Him the iniquity of us all. Out of the depths He cried, "My God, my God, why hast thou forsaken me"?

The three methods of preparing the Meal Offering may also be thought to convey an increasing intensity in the sufferings of Christ. The profound reality is that 'we may not know and we cannot tell what pains He had to bear'. We can follow Him only a little way in His sufferings for 'none of the ransomed ever knew how deep were the waters crossed, or how dark was the night that the Lord passed through ere He found the sheep that was lost'.

> *What He endured, no tongue can tell,*
> *To save our souls from wrath and hell.*

Many very specific instructions were given for the preparation of the Meal Offering. For instance, leaven and honey were never to be present and salt was never to be absent. (See Lev. 2:11-13.) The emphatic way in which these things are stated would seem to indicate that they have some very definite significance. Moreover the three things mentioned are repeatedly referred to throughout the scriptures.

(1) Leaven

Leaven universally symbolises evil. Jesus warned His disciples of the leaven of the Pharisees which is hypocrisy. What an insidious evil this is, and how common it is among Christians. Of course, hypocrisy will be more readily detected when it is found among those whose standard is nothing less than Christ Himself. A blind eye may be turned to hypocrisy in the world but invariably it will be noticed in the church. The Master also warned of the leaven of the Sadducees, which seems to represent rationalism and materialism. The Sadducees rejected any belief in an after life, they accepted only what the senses were able to discern.

Again the disciples were warned of the leaven of Herod. Since Herod stood at the head of the worldly power of that day the leaven of Herod seems to represent worldliness. In the epistles, Paul too, warned of leaven. He referred to the old leaven and to the leaven of malice and wickedness. (See1Cor.5:8.) Leaven always speaks of evil, (When rightly understood Matt.13:33 is no exception to this rule) its absence from the Meal Offering surely testifies to the flawless life of Him "who did no sin neither was guile found in His mouth." (1 Pet.2:22)

(2) Honey

Spelling out the reason for the absence of honey from the Meal Offering is not easy. The promised land is several times called a land flowing with milk and honey, and honey is also used as a figure for the word of God. (See Psa.81:16.) Our Lord was known as a man of sorrows and acquainted with grief, His was indeed a bitter cup, and it may be that this is symbolised by the absence of honey from the Meal Offering. On the other hand, a clue to this apparent enigma may perhaps be found in a proverb used among the ancients,

> It is not good to eat too much honey,
> Nor is it honourable to seek one's own honour.
> (Proverbs 25:27).

As honey is naturally pleasing to the palate so men are naturally inclined to seek their own advantage. The two basic instincts of the creature are self-protection and self-promotion. The self made man, even though he usually worships his maker, is held up as a pattern for all and especially for the young. The fact *that* he attained, rather than *how* he did so, is the all important thing. What matters is, that by fair means or foul, he succeeded in his goal of self-aggrandizement.

This is something our Saviour never did. On the contrary, we read that "Christ pleased not Himself." (Rom.15:3) It may be then, that these two, leaven and honey, represent the same thing but in different ways. Evil in its more disreputable and insidious forms is seen in the leaven, while honey, in this particular context, may represent evil in a more respectable form. But evil in all its guises was absent from the life of Him of whom the Meal Offering speaks. In the absolute sense of the term, His was a completely flawless life.

(3) Salt

A vital ingredient of every meal offering was salt. "You shall not allow the salt of the covenant of your God to be lacking from your Meal Offering." (Lev.2:13) Paul teaches us the significance of salt; he said "let your speech be always with grace, seasoned with salt." (Col.4:6) As people listened to the Saviour they sensed the seasoning in His words for "They marvelled at the gracious words that proceeded out of His mouth." (Luke 4:22) Others said, "Never man spoke like this man." (John7:46)

The main purpose of salt is to preserve from corruption, and its presence in the Meal Offering may remind us of the importance of hiding the word of Christ in our hearts, as the great preservative against sin in our lives. David said, "Thy word have I hid in my heart that I might not sin against thee." (Psa.119:11) The gracious words that proceeded out of His mouth revealed what was in Him, for it is out of the abundance of the heart, that the mouth speaks.

If the salt in the Meal Offering stands for the grace of our Lord Jesus Christ, it is significant that salt is never specified by amount in scripture. We speak of a pinch, a packet or a pound of salt, but not so the word of God. Similarily, grace is always spoken of as being without measure. We read of the grace of God, of the riches of His grace and of the exceeding riches of His grace.

Not only did grace and truth find their perfect balance in Christ but He was "full of grace and truth." (John 1:14) The Psalmist graphically pictured this when he said, "grace is poured into His lips." (Psa.45:2) Paul spoke of abundant grace and Peter used a telling phrase when he spoke of multiplied grace. Truly, the parallels are countless between type and antitype.

What an amazing life that was, which was laid down in death upon the cross. The world had never before witnessed a life to compare with the life of Jesus of Nazareth: nor has the like of it ever appeared again on the human stage. He stands alone. He is the incomparable Christ. Adjectives fail us in our attempts to portray the uniqueness of one who was "holy, harmless, undefiled, and separate from sinners." (Hebs .7:25) Beyond all contradiction, the laying down of His life for us was the substituting of "the just for the unjust, that He might bring us to God." (1Pet.3:18)

The three portions

It might be appropriate for us to pause at this point, and to note that the Meal Offering was divided into three parts or portions. To begin with, there was the memorial part which was burned on the altar. This was God's portion. It speaks of the satisfaction God found in the person of His Son. On three consecutive occasions He had spoken audibly, saying of Him, "this is my beloved Son in whom I am well pleased". And then, when the Son cried out on the cross, "It is finished" the Father, in effect, said "It is enough". The proof of this was seen on the third day when God raised Him from the dead. His ascension into heaven and His acceptance in the presence of God plainly declare that God is satisfied with Christ.

But there were two other parts to the Meal Offering. First the offerer himself took out his handful (v.2). This was an individual portion and it raises for us the important question, 'am I satisfied with Christ?' Thomas was satisfied with Christ for he said of Him, "my Lord and my God". John was satisfied with Him, for when he saw Him, he fell at His feet in adoring worship. Paul too was satisfied with Him for he said "To me to live is Christ". And again, "I count all things but loss for the excellency of the knowledge of Christ Jesus my Lord". Every true believer needs to allow this question to exercise his heart, 'am I truly satisfied with Him?'

The third part was a corporate portion. It belonged to the priestly family, to Aaron and his sons (v.10). They feasted upon it in the holy place. The corporate portion brings us to the fellowship of believers. Too many churches have become like the mixed multitude in the wilderness who had become dissatisfied with the manna. (See Numbers 11.) They lusted for the things they had formerly enjoyed in Egypt which, of course, always speaks to us of the world. "They tempted God in their heart by asking food according to their desire." (Psa.78:18) The immediate consequence for them was leanness of soul: and since their experience is recorded for our learning, the message must be that any church which is no longer satisfied with Christ, must surely be in a very parlous state indeed.

The New Meal Offering

Significantly, there are two Meal Offerings before us in the book of Leviticus. We have been considering the first or the old meal offering, but then another is mentioned in connection with the Feast of Pentecost. (See Lev.23:15-22.) It is termed the "New Meal Offering" and it consisted of two loaves of fine flour, baked with leaven. This new Meal Offering was closely identified with the Oblation of the Firstfruits mentioned alongside the old Meal Offering. (See Lev. 2:12-16.) Oblation was the word used for an offering that did not involve the shedding of blood.

At the beginning of the barley harvest a single sheaf, known as the sheaf of the firstfruits, was brought to the high priest to be waved before the Lord. This Oblation or offering of the firstfruits speaks of *the life of Christ risen*, the life that Jesus took again in resurrection. Paul declared, in what is generally recognised as the treatise par excellence on the resurrection, "Every man in his own order: Christ the firstfruits; afterward they that are Christ's at His coming." (1Cor.15:23)

But then after the firstfruits of the barley harvest, (fifty days later, to be precise) came the feast of Pentecost at which the firstfruits of the wheat harvest was offered. (Pentecost comes from the Greek word meaning fifty.) The offering presented on this occasion was the New Meal Offering, which took the form of two wave loaves. These two loaves taken together, seem to typify the bringing together of Jew and Gentile to form the church on the day of Pentecost. (See Acts 2.) The Oblation of the firstfruits (of the barley harvest) and the New Meal Offering (of the wheat harvest) therefore, are not identical, but they are very closely related.

41

The Firstfruits of the Barley Harvest

Just as the sheaf of the firstfruits (of the barley harvest) was the earnest of the harvest that was to follow, so the resurrection of Christ is the earnest of the resurrection of all who are Christ's at His coming. (1Cor.15:23) Two resurrections are revealed in scripture, one to life and the other to judgement. (See John 5:29.) Between the two resurrections a period of time extending to one thousand years will elapse, this period is often referred to as the time of our Lord's millennial kingdom. (See Rev.20:5.)

No true believer will have any part in the second resurrection. The Christian's hope is the coming of the Lord to the air to receive from the world His own. When He comes, He will bring with Him those who are now at home with the Lord. Their bodies will be raised in glory, and they will repossess those bodies in their resurrected and glorified form. At that point, we who are alive and remain will be changed, and together with the risen ones, we shall be caught up to meet the Lord in the air. And so shall we ever be with the Lord. (See 1Thess.4:13-18.)

The proper hope of the Christian, then, is a two fold hope. It is first the coming of the Lord, and then, our gathering together unto Him in the air. The guarantee of all this is the resurrection of Christ, for, "Now is Christ risen from [among] the dead and become the firstfruits of them that sleep." (1Cor.15:20) But more than that, the resurrection of Christ will itself be the pattern for the resurrection of His people at His coming again. Just as He was taken out from among the dead so His own will then be taken out while the rest of the dead are left to await the resurrection unto judgement.

The Firstfruits of the Wheat Harvest

When Jesus rose from the dead, He rose 'to be the Head over all things to the church' which is a new creation. This new creation is made up of all who are in Christ, who share in His risen life and who are joined to Him as members of His body. This mystical body (or church) of Christ, was formed at Pentecost by the coming of the Holy Spirit.(See Acts 2 & 1Cor.12:12,13.) The first members of this body were Jews but later Gentiles were added, and now in the body, "there is neither Jew nor Greek...for you are all one in Christ Jesus." (Gal.3:23) The fusing of believers from these two distinct and separate entities, to form the one body of Christ, seems to be what is foreshadowed in the two loaves which combined to make up the New Meal Offering.

What is it that unites all who are in Christ? What is the common bond? It can be nothing short of this, that they are sharers together in the risen life of Christ. To the believers at Colosse, Paul wrote, "For you are dead, and your life is hidden with Christ in God. When Christ, who is our life, shall appear, then shall you also appear with Him in glory." (Col.3:3,4) And so the two Meal Offerings seem to set forth respectively, the life of Christ personal, laid down in death, and the life of Christ Mystical, i.e. the life of Christ risen which is shared with all who belong to Him.

The scriptures have much to say on the subject of firstfruits. Should the reader wish to take up the subject, he might find it profitable to keep in mind that Christ Himself is the firstfruits of all who shall share in the first resurrection, [firstfruits of the barley harvest] and that the church of this dispensation is also 'a kind of firstfruits of His creatures.' [firstfruits of the wheat harvest] (James1:18). The apostle James seems to view the church as 'a kind of firstfruits' of the great harvest that is yet to be reaped among both Jews and Gentiles.

It would appear that when God's present purpose respecting the church is complete, He will take up again His purposes for national Israel and eventually "all Israel shall be saved." (Rom.11:26) And this will lead, in turn, to a spiritual harvest among the Gentile nations. (See Gen.12:3; Zech.14:16; Rev.21:24.)

On a practical note, believers are also reminded to "Honour the Lord with their substance, and with the firstfruits of all their increase." (Prov.3:9)

We have already stressed the absence of leaven from the first meal offering; but leaven was present in the second. How precise is the teaching of the types. Christ is sinless, but we are not. Alas, this side of Christ's appearing again, sin will ever be present with us. The leaven in the new Meal Offering is a reminder to us of the 'sin that dwelleth in us.' This side of glory, the church will never attain to perfection. Perfection is our goal, and we must be constantly reaching out towards it and striving after it. But the goal itself will only be reached when we reach home, and arrive in His presence.

Never offered alone

Finally we should note that the Meal Offering was never offered independently of the Burnt Offering. (See Num. 15:3,4 & 8,9.) These two offerings complimented each other. The reason for this must be that the sinless life of Christ was not of itself sufficient to accomplish atonement, it could not avail to put away sin. That perfect life had atoning efficacy only when it was poured out in death.

Atonement was accomplished only by the shedding of the precious blood of Christ. It was not the blood flowing in Immanuel's veins, but the blood shed for sinners that atoned for sins. The linking of these two offerings emphasies that, where there is an understanding of the truth of our acceptance on the ground of atonement, it will be followed by an ever deepening appreciation of the unique character of the life that was yielded up to death for us upon the cross.

> *Because the sinless Saviour died,*
> *My sinful soul is counted free;*
> *For God, the Just, is satisfied,*
> *To look on Him and pardon me.*

the peace offering

(Scripture Leviticus 3:1-17, 7:11-21.)

N.T. Fulfilment - "...having made peace through the blood of His cross..." "Therefore, being justified by faith, we have peace with God through our Lord Jesus Christ." (Col.1:20. Rom.5:1)

THE PEACE OFFERING HAS A RING ABOUT IT THAT STIRS OUR HEARTS. POLITICIANS AND STATESMEN MAKE MUCH ADO ABOUT THEIR STRIVINGS AFTER PEACE. BUT a cursory glance at any news-paper will show that the world of to-day finds peace as illusory as ever. Obviously, what is needed is a peace of an altogether different order. When Jesus died on Calvary He made another kind of peace. And what He accomplished is precisely what the Peace Offering had in view.

The Peace Offering differed from the two offerings we have already considered. There was no blood shedding in the Meal Offering while in this the blood is prominent. And then the Burnt Offering was for God alone; it was placed 'all on the altar'. But in the Peace Offering, God and man both have a portion. We must not think that because they differ that the offerings contradict one another. The offerings are complimentary, and taken together, they present a most magnificent patchwork of spiritual truth.

As the name suggests the Peace Offering implies that there is something wrong between God and man. All is not well, enmity has come in and man has become estranged from God. The cry of the ages was for a daysman, a go-between who could deal with the enmity; someone who could lay a hand upon God and a hand upon man and bring them together. (Job 9:33) And now at last a daysman has appeared in the person of God's Son, Jesus Christ our Lord. "For there is one mediator between God and men, the man Christ Jesus, who gave Himself a ransom for all." (1Tim.2:5,6) And in this unique capacity the Lord Jesus is brought before us in the Peace Offering.

Reconciliation, in biblical terms, does not signify a compromise by both parties. In fact, God is never said to be reconciled. The word itself means 'to change completely' and the scriptures clearly teach that "God was in Christ reconciling [changing completely] the world unto Himself." (2 Cor. 5:19) Through the death of Christ, the position of the world in relation to God is completely different from what it would have been had Christ not died. Apart from the cross, this lost world must have remained forever lost, but since Christ has died there is salvation for a lost world, a salvation that is experienced by all who avail themselves of it, through individual and personal faith in Christ. (See 2 Cor. 5:20,21.)

It is at this point we are able to appreciate the significance of the Peace Offering. The precise purpose for which it was brought was not to make atonement or even to achieve peace; it was rather by way of response to such blessing already received. The Peace Offering was an expression of the offerer's thanksgiving for peace already enjoyed. It was presented as a token of fellowship enjoyed both with the Lord and with His people.

The Peace Offering may have been taken from the herd or from the flock. In either case blood had to be shed. Again the truth is underlined: it was not the life that Jesus lived that saved, it was that life laid down in death as a sacrifice for sin. The victim had to be without blemish, symbolic of the perfection of Christ. And yet something more was needed, the victim must be slain. And so we read that peace was made through His blood, shed on the cross. (Col.1:20) The gospel proclaims peace by Jesus Christ, a peace that could only be procured by the shedding of His most precious blood.

The Meaning of Peace

But the Peace Offering has much more in view than simply the removing of enmity between God and man. While this is implicit, it is by no means the primary thought. This offering envisages a restoration of the fellowship which was broken by sin; so that man might again walk with God, learn His mind and find pleasure in doing His will. "The word *peace* has a shade of meaning in scripture, not usually attached to it in ordinary use. Generally it signifies a cessation of hostilities and the absence of discord. But in scripture it means much more; here its predominant idea is of prosperity and happiness." (See Seiss, The Gospel in Leviticus, p 64.)

In Israel, the bringing of the Peace Offering was always a happy time for it was a time of fellowship with the Lord and with His people. It was an occasion, joyous above all others. A notable instance of this was at the dedication of the Temple. "Solomon sacrificed Peace Offerings unto the Lord, two and twenty thousand oxen, and one hundred and twenty thousand sheep." And then, when he sent the people away on the eighth day, we are told, "they blessed the king and went unto their tents joyful and glad of heart." (1Kings 8:63, 66) In its historical setting, the Peace Offering was presented on those occasions when the godly of Israel desired to express their sense of communion with the Lord, and with all those who shared that sense of communion with them.

Fellowship defined

But true fellowship is not simply a matter of cultivating happy frames and feelings. The very essence of Christian fellowship is experienced when believers find a common joy and delight in Christ. There are two dimensions to this fellowship. On the one hand it is *human:* John's first epistle was written "that you might have fellowship with us." And then on the other hand it is *divine,* for John added, "our fellowship is with the Father and with His Son Jesus Christ." (1John 1:3)

Fellowship is therefore, much more than just a number of people of similar temperament, background or outlook enjoying happy times together. On the contrary, true fellowship finds greater opportunity for expression in dark and difficult days. And even then Christian fellowship is enjoyed when believers share, one with another and with the Father, their common portion in Christ. Admittedly we can never rise to the level of the Father's thoughts concerning His Son. But just as Christ is the object of the Father's delight, so when He becomes our object too, we enjoy communion with the Father, for then we are sharing together our common portion in Christ.

Probably the most precious Old Testament anticipation of this fellowship was when the people brought their Peace Offerings. Indeed, the Lord may have had this in mind when He called to the Christians at Laodicea, "Behold, I stand at the door, and knock; if any man hear my voice, and open the door, *I will come in to him, and will sup with him, and he with me.*" (Rev.3:20) Alas, when those words were spoken the Lord was looking in from the outside. How we need to restore to the Lord His rightful place in the midst of His people!

Two aspects of Calvary

The Peace Offering differed from the Burnt Offering in that it was divided into two parts, there was a part for God and a part for man. The Burnt Offering was all for God, it was placed 'all on the altar'. And yet the two Offerings are closely allied, for that part of the Peace Offering which was burned on the altar, was burned upon the Burnt Sacrifice (v.5). We must always maintain these two aspects of Christ's death upon the cross.

There is a Godward aspect to Calvary. "Christ...has given Himself...an offering and a sacrifice to God for a sweet smelling savour." (Eph.5:2) And again, "Christ, through the eternal Spirit offered Himself without spot to God." (Hebs.9:14) But there is also a manward aspect which is indicated in such scriptures as "Christ died for the ungodly" and "Christ died for us." (Rom.5:6,8) John wrote, "He is the propitiation [satisfaction] for our sins, and not for ours only, but also for the sins of the whole world." (1John 2:2)

It should be noted that it was the inward parts of the sacrifice that were burned on the altar. This seems to symbolise the inner springs that motivated the Saviour in all that He did. Every inward thought and desire was tested in the fire of divine holiness and all was found to be a sweet savour unto the Lord. That part burned on the altar is specifically said to have furnished "Food...unto Jehovah" (Lev.3:11). To view Calvary in terms of what the Jews did, or what the Romans did, or what the soldiers did, is to be much too superficial. Besides reflecting upon those judgement scenes, we need to ponder long and deeply what it meant to the heart of God, that the Lord Jesus was obedient unto death.

We often dwell on the manward or subjective side of Calvary, and this is good, for it promotes praise. But there is something even better. We should dwell more and more on the Godward side of the cross for this promotes worship, and worship is the highest exercise in which the human spirit can engage. We might say that when Christ came, He came seeking sinners, but to-day the Father comes seeking worshippers. "True worshippers, worship the Father in spirit and in truth; and the Father seeks such to worship Him." (John 4:23)

Many kinds of Peace

The word translated *peace* in 'peace-offering' is a plural word. It means, all kinds of peace or *peace upon peace*. Where the plural is used in this way it seems to convey the idea of fullness and completeness. Take, for example, the reference to "the righteousness (lit. righteousnesses) of the saints." (Rev.19:8) The phrase takes in all the righteous acts of believer's which, like individual threads woven together, will combine to make up the wedding dress of the bride of Christ at the marriage supper of the Lamb. In His death, Christ secured all kinds of peace for us, peace of heart, of mind and of conscience. And all kinds of peace seem to be involved in the Pauline benediction, "Now the Lord of peace Himself give you peace always by all means." (2Thess.3:16)

(1) Personal

In the New Testament, peace is referred to in a number of senses. In its individual aspect we read, "Therefore, being justified by faith, we have peace with God through our Lord Jesus Christ." (Rom 5:1) Because God was in Christ reconciling the world unto Himself, a ground has now been established upon which believing sinners can be reconciled to God. And being reconciled, it is their happy portion to enjoy peace with God. The text quoted is sometimes rendered, "Let us have [or Let us enjoy] peace with God."

> *A mind at perfect peace with God;*
> *Oh what a word is this!*
> *A sinner reconciled through blood;*
> *This, this indeed is peace!*

(2) Corporate

But peace is also viewed in a corporate sense. "For He is our peace, who has made both one, and has broken down the middle wall of partition between us...to make in Himself of two, one new man, so making peace. And that He might reconcile both unto God in one body by the cross, having slain the enmity thereby." (Eph.2:14-16) The extended passage from which this quotation is taken reveals how believing Jews and believing Gentiles have been brought together in the 'body of Christ' to share with one another in the enjoyment of the peace that was established in the cross.

And then as a general rule and as a principle of daily living, we are exhorted, as much as lies within us to live at peace with all men. But the kind of peace Paul wrote about is not only different, it is much more. Here we have people from two violently opposed backgrounds and of widely differing national and cultural temperaments finding reconciliation through a common interest and faith in Christ.

In like manner, since we became united to Christ, and as a direct result, we find ourselves at one with those who are Christ's. Believers are not simply a collection of individuals, they are members one of another, for, as we noted in our last chapter, they are members together in the body of Christ. And so peace must be seen in both a vertical sense, peace with God, and in a horizontal sense, peace with all who love the Saviour's name, and, so far as in us lies, with all men.

(2) Regulative

A variation on this theme is the exhortation, "Let the peace of God (Christ *r.s.v.*) rule in your hearts." (Col.3:15) Jesus said, "Peace I leave with you, my peace I give unto you." (John 14:27) At conversion the believer not only enters into an objective standing, described as *peace with God*; he also receives a subjective *peace of God* which is to rule in his heart. To 'rule' here means to umpire or referee. The word conveys the idea of arbitration, and its outworking may take several forms.

Just as in a game of football, when a foul is committed, the referee blows his whistle and play is halted until the wrong has been put right, so a disturbance of peace in his heart is a signal to the Christian that something contrary to the mind of Christ has been entered into his life. Peace will only be resumed when the wrong is dealt with. Again, perhaps a decision, surrounded by perplexity and anxiety, has had to be made, the peace of God ruling in his heart will reassure the believer when the decision is a right one. Conversely, a persistent unhappiness with a given decision should alert the believer and cause him to think again.

The plural 'in your hearts' would seem to indicate that there is a corporate aspect to this matter as well. When differences threaten to divide believers, then the peace of God must be allowed to arbitrate, for we are urged "to keep the unity of the Spirit in the bond of peace." (Eph.4:3) It is always a reproach to the name of Christ when the apparent unity among believers is nothing more than some forced or convenient tolerance.

(4) Millennial

But peace is also proclaimed in a millennial sense. To the Colossians Paul wrote, "And having made peace through the blood of His cross...to reconcile all things unto Himself...whether they be things in earth, or things in heaven." (Col.1:20) This anticipates a day that has clearly not yet arrived. Apart from Christ, "There is no peace, says my God, to the wicked," (Isa.57:21) but a day will come when earth will be brought into harmony with heaven, and the will of God will be done in earth as it is in heaven. In that day, "The work of righteousness shall be peace; and the effect of righteousness, quietness and assurance forever." (Isa.32:17)

But no matter how many aspects there may be to peace, the ground of it is always the same. It is "the blood of His cross." (Col.1:20) In the beginning, Abel acknowledged that only in the blood of the slain Lamb, could he find a ground for peace with God. The Peace Offering is termed a sacrifice, and it teaches that the blood of sacrifice is still the only ground of peace with God.

The Peace Offering bids us look away from ourselves and our own works, to 'Him who sealed our pardon with His blood' and to rest by faith on what He has done.

> *I hear the words of love,*
> *I gaze upon the blood,*
> *I see the mighty sacrifice,*
> *And I have peace with God.*

Why a Peace Offering?

But someone might ask, why should a Peace Offering have been brought in the first place? And especially since the offerer, in all probability, was already one of the elect race. The answer to that question is found in what is known as 'the law of the peace offerings'. This law was addressed, not to the people as a whole but to Aaron and his sons. It conveyed additional instructions to the officiating priest to guide him in his handling of the offerings.

Let us assume that a person was conscious of having been blessed in some signal way; and now to show his gratitude to God, he brings a Peace Offering as an offering of thanksgiving. Or, on the other hand, he might wish to commit himself to some definite service for the Lord. In which case his Peace Offering would be for a vow, it would be a tangible token of his pledge and commitment to the Lord. (See Lev.7:12&16.)

These two possibilities seem to cover the whole range of Christian exercise; the first being purely objective and the second subjective. If we relate them to the communion service, these two things sum up what it is all about. Sometimes it is said that the Lord's Supper is nothing more than a memorial of thanksgiving. That it is this, cannot be questioned, but it must surely be more. In partaking of the bread and wine we are also affirming afresh our love and loyalty to our Saviour. This is what is implied in the exhortation, "Let a man examine himself, and so let him eat." The absence of this subjective side of the exercise must devalue the ordinance itself and greatly impoverish our observance of it.

Sometimes the supper is called a *sacrament*. This word comes from the Latin 'sacramentum', which was the oath of allegiance to the Emperor, taken by a Roman soldier when he enlisted in the army. The Lord's Supper should be thought of as our sacramentum. In it we not only give thanks, but we also give ourselves anew to Him who gave Himself for us.

Enjoying the Peace Offering

At first sight it might seem a strange injunction that the flesh of the peace offering was to be eaten on the same day that it was offered. (Lev.7:15) This insistence on such a close connection between the actual offering of the sacrifice, and the consuming of it, must have some spiritual significance. A very important principle may be contained in this proviso. In practical terms, the giving of thanks may take place in a moment, while the performance of a vow may require some time; in such an event the Peace Offering could be held over for a second day, but no longer. Any of it that remained over to the third day was burned. (Lev.7:16,17)

Every servant of Christ should note well this close connection between the eating of the Peace Offering, and the offering of it. In the Christian life it is so important for us to be constrained by the love of Christ in all that we do. How He gave Himself for us should be the spring of our inspiration, both in the giving of thanks and in the giving of ourselves. We love Him, said John, because He first loved us. People are often moved to action by harrowing tales of human suffering, but the compelling and motivating force in the Christian life must always be the love of Christ.

Just as on the first passover; the people sheltered beneath the sprinkled blood, on the same night as they feasted on the lamb roast with fire, so the sacrifice of the Peace Offering and the eating of it went together. The enjoyment of fellowship with the Lord can never be divorced from the work of the cross upon which it has been established. Furthermore, just as the manna was enjoyed on the same day as it came down from heaven, so we need to experience a fresh, daily feasting upon Christ, for a previous experience of Him will not do for the peculiar needs of each new day.

In a day of easy going, comfortable Christianity, we should also ponder deeply the strict prohibition on allowing the Peace Offering to remain over to the third day. "But the remainder of the flesh of the sacrifice on the third day shall be burned with fire. And if any...be eaten at all on the third day, it shall not be accepted...it shall be an abomination." (Lev.7:17,18) Our service may be applauded by many, it may have the approbation of the church, but if it is separated from Christ and if it is engaged in apart from Him, it is only an abomination in the sight of God. There can never be an adequate substitute for a fresh and up-to-the-minute experience of Christ.

Christian Corporateness

A practical point might be raised here. If the Peace Offering was a bullock from the herd, how could the offerer consume it in one or two days? Of course this was quite impossible, nor was he required even to attempt such a thing. The idea was that he would call his friends and neighbours and, in happy fellowship, they would together feast upon the Peace Offering. The very offering which foreshadowed how, in the person of our Lord Jesus Christ, "mercy and truth are met together; and righteousness and peace have kissed each other" (Psa. 85:10).

This point was graphically illustrated in some of the parables. For instance, when the shepherd found his lost sheep, when the woman found her lost coin, and when the father found his lost son, what did they do? They called together their friends and neighbours and said, "rejoice with me for I have found the thing that was lost." (See Luke 15.) In the same way, we must always be mindful of the important part played by the fellowship of other believers in developing Christian experience. The Peace Offering is a vivid illustration of the communion of saints, of the corporate nature of Christianity, of believers together finding a common delight and enjoyment in the person and work of the Lord Jesus Christ.

Communion is not a matter of religious frames and feelings; it is certainly not a preoccupation with ourselves, even in our more pious moments. There can be no true communion with God or with His people except on the ground of that one supreme sacrifice of Calvary, where our Lord Jesus Christ made peace through the blood of His cross. When meaningfully observed, the Lord's Supper speaks powerfully to our hearts of these things. The exercise is aptly called the communion service for at His table we are together occupied with the infinite love and grace of Christ who, in giving Himself, comprehensively expressed the heart of God toward us.

Christian fellowship is also a very practical matter especially when it comes to the cultivation and exercise of a ministry of prayer. Few Christians can testify to finding individual prayer easy. We soon become like Moses when he went up into the mount to pray: he grew weary and allowed his hands to hang down. But then Aaron and Hur came alongside, now there were *two or three*, and they upheld his hands till the going down of the sun: long enough for Joshua to defeat Amalek army in the valley. (See.Ex.17:8-16.)

And what a difference fellowship with other believers can make in the exercise of the ministry of prayer. As we gather together in the place of corporate prayer and join with others, of kindred spirit, who really believe that God hears and answers prayer, we are able to sing with more meaning and certainly with more honesty,

> *Oh the pure delight of a single hour,*
> *That before thy throne I spend;*
> *When I kneel in prayer, and with thee my God,*
> *I commune as friend with friend.*

The Beauty of Holiness

Having said all that, however, we still have to acknowledge that spiritual communion is a very delicate plant. It can be easily hindered and even marred. We are told that if "the flesh [of the Peace Offering] touched any unclean thing it shall not be eaten; it shall be burned with fire." (Lev.7:19) The third commandment says "Thou shalt not take the name of the Lord thy God in vain." (Ex: 20:7) This is usually interpreted to mean the use of unseemly language, but it probably has a meaning much nearer to us than that. Christians bear the name of Christ, and when in our persons, we link that name with any uncleanness, then we are in violation of the third commandment.

Nor can Christian fellowship be taken for granted. On the contrary, it has to be both carefully cultivated and jealously guarded. There are things not lawful for a Christian even to touch. Things which, if allowed, will spoil his enjoyment of any kind of meaningful fellowship. 'Little foxes spoil the vine' and little sins often ruin the communion of believers. Church elders have a duty to guard the public testimony of the house of God, and individual believers have as their first charge the responsibility of maintaining right personal relations with the Lord and with His people.

There are three ways in which the need for holiness in divine things is brought home to us by the law of the Peace Offering. In the first place, when this sacrifice was offered, both *unleavened* cakes and *leavened* cakes were offered with it. We always have to recognise as a fact, that while in the Lord there is purity, there is sin in us. This is symbolised by the absence of leaven in the one case and the presence of it in the other, for leaven in scripture is a symbol of sin. Christian fellowship therefore, is impossible if a prior requirement for it is perfection in Christians. Secondly, there is a moral separation from evil which we must always maintain. "If we say that we have fellowship with Him, and walk in darkness, we lie, and do not the truth" (1John 1:6).

And then in the third place, the need for holiness of life, both positively and negatively, is restated in the law of the Peace Offering. "All who are clean shall eat thereof. But the soul that eateth ... having his uncleanness upon him shall be cut off from his people." (Lev 7:19,20) The word *upon* should be noted in this statement. The Lord Jesus had no sin *in* Him but He took our sins *upon* Him. In consequence, believers, while they have sin *in* them, have now no sin *upon* them. "The blood of Jesus Christ, God's Son, cleanseth us from all sin." (1John 1:7)

When all this is analysed it surely teaches that anyone who shares in Christian fellowship in any significant way is like the Israelite who came bringing his Peace Offering. He is saying, in effect, that while seeking to maintain a moral separation from evil, he is in himself a poor sinner, sin is in his very nature, but because of the cleansing blood, he has now no sin upon him. The basis of Christian fellowship therefore, is not some nicety of interpretation, nor is it a doctrinaire acceptance of what may simply be an unbalanced emphasis upon only one aspect of truth. Our fellowship rests entirely upon the blood of Jesus and a commitment to a moral separation from everything clearly inconsistent with that precious blood.

The love and power of Christ

The Peace Offering may have been taken from the herd or from the flock and in either case it could have been a male or a female. But in every case, when the portions were divided, the breast was given to the priests, to Aaron and his sons; and the right shoulder was given as a special portion to the officiating priest. All believers in this dispensation are priests unto God. We are "a holy priesthood" and "a royal priesthood." (1Pet.2:5,9) It is our holy privilege to meditate upon Christ, upon His love and upon His power. In doing so we are like the priests of old as they feasted on the breast and the right shoulder of the Peace Offering.

We see the right shoulder, the symbol of strength, in Paul's first prayer for the Ephesians. He prayed that they might know "what is the exceeding greatness of His power toward us who believe." (Eph.1:19) Then in his second prayer, it is the breast of the Peace Offering that comes into view, for now he prays that they might know "the love of Christ, which passes knowledge." (Eph.3:19) Oh to rest more fully in the knowledge that He who loved us, loves us still. And that His power is such that He is able to perform everything that, in love, He has purposed for us.

Finally, we might note that in the law of the offerings the Peace Offering is mentioned last, whereas in the classification of the offerings it is listed third. Its third place means that there were two on either side of it, making the Peace Offering central. We know that the ministry of reconciliation, which is the blessed reality of which the Peace Offering was only a shadow, is the core truth of the gospel. Coming last in the law of the offerings it seems to emphasise that the blessed result and ultimate goal of that mighty work, which all the offerings taken together portray, is that sinners who believe might be reconciled to God.

A mind at perfect peace with God,
Oh what a word is this,
A sinner reconciled through blood,
This indeed is peace.

the sin offering

(Scripture Leviticus 4:1-35, 6:24-30.)

N.T. Fulfilment - "God commends His love toward us in that, while we were yet sinners, Christ died for us." (Rom.5:8)

OF THE FIVE PRINCIPLE OFFERINGS IN THE LEVITICAL SYSTEM, THE LAST TWO WERE THE SIN OFFERING AND THE TRESPASS OFFERING AND THESE WERE SOMEWHAT different from the others. They were not said to be sweet savour offerings. The reason for this appears to be that, whereas the other offerings were voluntary, God demanded the Sin and Trespass Offerings. In addition, of course, as their names indicate, these offerings we directly concerned with the question of sin.

There are two basic thoughts associated with the offering of sacrifice in scripture. In the first place, there is the idea of appeasement. God is *light* as well as *love*. Divine holiness was outraged by man's sin and for that sin no man could give to God a satisfaction. But Jesus came, and in the fullness of time He presented Himself to God a sacrifice for sins. By that mighty sacrifice, He settled every claim of God's outraged holiness and, at the same time, He established a completely righteous ground upon which sinful man might be reconciled to God.

The second idea behind the sacrifices is worship, praise and thanksgiving. It is because of the atonement accomplished by Christ's one sacrifice for sins, that the believer is now able to offer a sacrifice of praise to God, the fruit of his lips giving thanks to His name. (Hebs.13:15) These two ideas are enshrined in the two different kinds of offerings. While the second idea is expressed in the offerings we have already dealt with, the sweet savour offerings, the first is defined in the two offerings that remain for us now to consider.

As their names suggest, the two remaining offerings were sacrifices for sin. The precise difference between them is admittedly a little difficult to define. They are not identical, and yet they are closely related for we read, "as the Sin Offering is, so is the Trespass Offering; there is one law for them." (Lev.7:7) In broad terms we might say that the former was concerned with the sinner as a person, while the latter had to do with the sins he had committed.

First - the Sin Offering

It is helpful to bear in mind that when the sacrifices were formulated into a system, the Sin Offering was the first to be offered. Before then all the sacrifices were probably Burnt Offerings, but when the Levitical system was introduced and the various sacrifices were distinguished, the Sin Offering came first before all the others.

As earlier noted, a moments reflection will show that in point of time, the events of Leviticus chapters one to seven (where the details of all the offerings are recorded) came after the events of chapters eight and nine. The consecration and appointment of Aaron and his sons necessarily preceded the service they were appointed to fulfil. That service was principally to offer sacrifice. And so it was that on the day of their consecration, their first duty was to bring a Sin Offering. (Lev.8:14)

This is in harmony with our own experience. When we first came to Christ the paramount question that pressed upon us was the question of our sins. The truth proclaimed in the offerings already considered probably did not even cross our minds. But having experienced the forgiveness of sins through faith in Jesus Christ, we can now follow on to know Him, we can grow in the knowledge of Christ, and learn Him as He is seen in the other offerings.

It is interesting to note that when the Sin Offering was for a priest who had sinned, three things were done with the blood of the offering. It was first sprinkled seven times before the Lord, before the veil of the sanctuary. Then it was put upon the horns of the Golden Altar and finally the remainder of the blood was poured out at the bottom of the altar of sacrifice, the Brazen Altar. These three actions symbolise how the blood of Christ has satisfied God, by it a righteous basis has been laid on which man may approach God and it also lies at the foundation of all God's dealings with men.

What Sin is

The first thing to which the inspired record calls attention is the way in which sin is viewed when looked at from the standpoint of the Sin Offering. "If a soul shall sin against any of the commandments of the Lord concerning things which ought not to be done, and shall do against any of them..." (Lev.4:2) Sin is here viewed as a transgression of the revealed will of God, a rejection of His word, a rebellion against His authority, and as an assault against His throne. "Sin is a transgression of the law." (1John 3:4)

(1) From Adam to Moses

While death reigned during the period between Adam and Moses, no one during that time had sinned in exactly the same way as Adam had sinned. Adam had transgressed a clearly defined and specifically prescribed law. It was only when the moral law was given to Moses, that sin assumed the peculiar character that law gives it. Law gives sin an added dimension, it gives it the character of transgression. It shows sin to be a revolt against the Creator, to whom the creature is at all times responsible. Under law therefore, sin is not just an offence, it is also a transgression. Paul tells us that "death reigned from Adam to Moses, even over them that had not sinned after the similitude of Adam's transgression." (Rom.5:14)

Low views of sin mean low views of God. And with no fear of God before their eyes, fools make a mock of sin. But the Sin Offering treats sin as being exceedingly sinful, it postulates sin at its worst. Sin is here faced up to in its most crimson and scarlet hues. In God's sight all sin is as scarlet, it is red like crimson. And that is how God met sin at Calvary when "He made the Lord Jesus, who knew no sin, to be sin for us." (2Cor.5:21) The law's just sentence reads, "The soul that sins shall die." (Ez.18:20) But God, in grace, provided a sinless substitute to die in the sinners place. Our Sin Offering is the Lord Jesus Christ who died for us, even while we were yet sinners.

(2) From Moses to Christ

In Old Testament times sin found its provisional answer in the Sin Offering, but those ancient sacrifices merely covered over the problem, they did not solve it. The conscience of the offerer might have been purged for a while, reflecting the value of the offering he brought. But the repetitive nature of those sacrifices also had the effect of bringing to the offerers mind a consciousness of his former sins. The full and final answer to the problem of sin was only provided when Jesus died on the cross of Calvary. For Christ has obtained eternal redemption for us.

> *Calvary covers it all, my past with its sin and shame,*
> *My guilt and despair, Jesus took on Him there,*
> *And Calvary covers it all.*

It was the anticipation of Calvary that enabled Isaiah to proclaim, "though your sins be as scarlet, they shall be as white as snow; though they be red like crimson, they shall be as wool." (Isa.1:18) And because of Calvary the apostle can assure us that "the blood of Jesus Christ, God's Son, cleanseth us from all sin." (1John1:7) Everything that required to be done for the justification of guilty sinners, was done, when Jesus bled and died, and now there remains no more to be done. Our great Sin Offering is the complete, root and branch, answer to the complex question of human sin.

Ignorance

But the sin for which the Sin Offering was provided is described as sin committed through ignorance. (Lev.4:2) This introduces us to a very wonderful aspect of the grace of God. "Almost all things are by the law purged with blood." (Hebs.9:22) The stress should be placed on the word *almost*. There is no provision anywhere in the Bible for wilful sin. But since the blood of Jesus has been shed for all, we are each responsible to avail ourselves of its worth. Wilful failure to do so exposes us to the solemn and certain judgement of God.

The wilful sinner is the person who is enlightened as to his need and his danger, who has been made aware of the truth of the gospel, and who then categorically refuses to acknowledge the Lord Jesus in any personal way. That individual, having no saving interest in the precious blood, is without hope, not only in time but for all eternity. "For if we sin wilfully after we have received the knowledge of the truth, there remains no more sacrifice for sins, but a certain fearful looking for of judgement and fiery indignation." (Hebs.10:26,27)

The Forgiveness of God

As the offspring of fallen parents, we are fallen creatures who cannot stop from sinning. But in marvellous grace, God has attributed the sins we have committed, our secret sins and our scarlet sins, to the ignorance that is in us by nature. In doing this

He has effectively brought all our sins within the range of His pardoning grace. Consequently we may now be forgiven, and more to the point, since Christ has died, we may be righteously forgiven. Because of Calvary, "God can be just, and at the same time the justifier of him who believes in Jesus." (Rom.3:26)

There are several illustrations of this in The New Testament. Take, for example, our Lord's first word from the cross. He prayed for the soldiers who nailed Him to the tree, "Father forgive them; for they know not what they do." (Luke 23:34) Or again, take Paul the apostle, reflecting on his own conversion, he wrote, "I obtained mercy, because I did it ignorantly in unbelief." (1Tim.1:13) By our standards, what was done in both instances, was done consciously and with malice; and yet, in matchless grace and tender mercy, God put it all down to the ignorance that was in them by nature, thus bringing the persons concerned within the range of His forgiving love and pardoning grace.

At the same time, we must not overlook the important fact that *ignorance* implies that the atonement, when it was made, was made according to God's estimate of the sin committed. The offender might have excused himself on the ground of ignorance but God makes no excuse or allowance for sin. Sin must be judged, and when that judgement fell upon Christ, the atonement which was accomplished reached beyond the extent to which the sinner's conscience felt it's guilt; it reached up to heaven itself and met all the requirements of God's exalted throne.

Privilege and Responsibility

Even a casual reading of Lev.4 impresses on the mind that God distinguished between the sins of an anointed priest and the sins of one of the congregation. He put a similar difference between sins committed by a ruler and those committed by one of the common people. The question immediately arises, since sin is sin, how can a righteous God discriminate in this way? Why should the sins of one of the common people be treated separately from the sins of a ruler, or even of an anointed priest?

There are two ways in which this question must be approached. In the first place, the difference between the various persons identified is one of privilege and therefore it is also one of responsibility. Greater privilege always carries greater responsibility. And since God is righteous, His judgements require and He must insist that both responsibility and privilege, according to their measure, be taken into take account.

Conclusive confirmation of this is found in the Saviour's own words. He upbraided the cities wherein most of His mighty works were done, because they repented not. "Woe unto you Chorazin! Woe unto you Bethsaida! For if the mighty works which were done in you, had been done in Tyre and Sidon, they would have repented long ago in sackcloth and ashes." Then He added, "But I say unto you, It shall be more tolerable for Tyre and Sidon at the day of judgement than for you." "And thou, Capernaum, who are exalted to heaven, you shall be brought down to hell; for if the mighty works, which have been done in you, had been done in Sodom, it would have remained to this day. But I say unto you, that it shall be more tolerable for the land of Sodom in the day of judgement, than for you." (Matt.11:20-24)

This basic principle is universal in its application; and those who live in lands accustomed to the light of the gospel need to be solemnly reminded of it. We are forced to admit, and sometimes in circumstances that embarrass the faithful, that many who boast a clear understanding of the truth of God, often appear the most careless in applying that same truth to themselves.

Only one Sin Offering

But the question we have posed must be looked at in another way as well. It is true that distinctions are made between the various types of sinners assumed in Lev.4; yet in every case the answer to their sins is one and the same, it is the Sin Offering. That single provision made for sin, points us forward to Christ, our great Sin Offering who alone is our Saviour. A deliberate rejection of that single provision by one who knows the way, exposes that person to judgement. Where mercy is rejected judgement must surely fall, because after Christ there is no further sacrifice for sins. (See Hebs.10:26.)

Once for ever

It is a startling fact that not all the Sin-Offerings sacrificed across the many years of the Levitical system served to put away sins, they merely covered them over until Christ should come. This was true even when the Sin Offerings were combined with all their associated sacrifices; and in one day, at the dedication of the Temple, Solomon offered twenty two thousand oxen and one hundred and twenty thousand sheep. (See 2Chron.7:5.)

But in the fullness of the time, God sent forth His Son. The Lord Jesus was identified by John the Baptist as "the Lamb of God, who *takes away* the sin of the world" (John 1:29). And Peter wrote of Him in His death, He "*bore our sins in His own body* on the tree" (1Pet.2:24). In addition, there is the compelling testimony of the epistle to the Hebrews, where the writer, after arguing that the very repetition of those Old Testament sacrifices proved their inadequacy, goes on to say, "But this man, after He had offered *one sacrifice for sins forever*, sat down on the right hand of God" (Hebs.10:12).

Not all the blood of beasts, on Jewish altars slain,
Could give the guilty conscience peace,
Or wash away the stain.
But Christ the heavenly Lamb, takes all our sins away;
A sacrifice of nobler name, and richer blood than they.

One for All

In practical terms this means that from the highest to the lowest, from the most learned to the most illiterate, from the richest to the poorest, all must discover that there is only one answer to the problem of their sins. Christ alone is the answer. He is the divinely provided Sin Offering.

> *'Nothing can for sin atone,*
> *Nothing but the blood of Jesus.'*

To sum up we might note two things. Firstly, the righteousness of God requires that in all His judgements, God must take account of people's privileges as well as of their responsibilities; and, secondly, that in wondrous grace He has provided, in the person of His Son, a Saviour for all regardless of their status in life. It follows therefore, that the gospel of salvation is never to be proclaimed on the basis of class or colour, nor on the basis of privilege or the lack of it, but simply and always on the basis of human need. "This is a faithful saying and worthy of all acceptation, that Christ Jesus came into the world to save sinners." (1Tim.1:15)

The only fitness God requires of us is a recognition of our true state, that we are undeserving sinners in His sight. Nor does our estate need to be proven for our own hearts themselves condemn us. Should our position in society lead us to think of ourselves as one of the common people, or as a prince or even as an anointed priest, we must each come before God as a poor sinner and claim the divinely provided Sin Offering, even Jesus, as our own. With bibical assurance we are able to proclaim that one who comes on this ground will never be denied.

The Blood and the Body

What was done respectively, with the blood and the body of the sacrifice, however, probably conveys the central thought in the Sin-Offering. The blood was brought within, inside the Veil; the body was burned without, outside the camp. These instructions, it should be noted, were carried out under the very strict conditions laid down in Levitical law and signified the severity of God's judgement upon sin.

The blood was sprinkled seven times before the Lord, before the veil of the sanctuary. On the great day of atonement it was carried within the veil itself and sprinkled both before and on the mercy-seat, thus signifying God's acceptance of the sacrifice. The body, apart from the fat, was burned outside the camp. The ashes that remained were then taken aside to a 'clean place' reminding us of how the sacred body of the Lord Jesus was taken down from the cross and laid in Joseph's new tomb, in which no man before had been laid.

Together these two things clearly set forth the two aspects of our identification with Christ. In the case of the burnt offering the offerer literally pressed his hands upon the victims head and he did the same in the matter of the Sin Offering. It was a quite definite and deliberate act. Our identification with Christ must be like that. It is no half hearted commitment that leads us to confess Him, "My Lord and my God." From that point we have been identified with Him inside the veil, in His acceptance before God. "We are accepted in the Beloved." (Eph. 1:4) We do not need to wait until we reach the other side to be assured of this; Christ is accepted in Heaven and we are in Him. And so we rejoice in our acceptance before God as a present reality.

But if the bringing of the blood of the Sin Offering within the veil speaks of our identification with Christ in His acceptance before God, the body burned without, outside the camp, speaks of our identification with Him in His rejection before men. Our Lord was crucified without the city. Terms such as the outside place, or outside the camp, are terms that tell of rejection. "He came unto His own and His own received Him not." (John 1:11) And when the people to whom He came cried, "We will not have this man to reign over us," it was inevitable that the only place for Him was the outside place.

Identification with Christ

Since 'the servant is not greater than his master' it follows, that our place is to be on the Lord's side, identifiying ourselves with Him in His rejection before men. This will not be a popular course, it may even be a costly one, but it is the correlative of our identification with Him in His acceptance before God. These two things are the two sides of a very wonderful truth. Moreover, to stand with Him in His rejection is surely an evidence, if not the ultimate proof, of our saving interest in His acceptance.

Should any be tempted to think that this interpretation of the Sin Offering is strained they have only to refer to the teaching of the Hebrew epistle. "The bodies of those beasts, whose blood is brought into the sanctuary by the High Priest for sin, are burned outside the camp. Wherefore Jesus also, that He might sanctify the people with His own blood, suffered without the gate. Let us go forth, therefore, unto Him outside the camp, bearing His reproach." (Hebs.13:11)

In the law of the Sin Offering there are two further things we might note for our profit. The first is this, "Whatsoever shall touch the flesh of the Sin Offering shall be holy." (Lev.6:27) Such was the power in the Sin Offering, everything coming into contact with it, and from the very moment of contact, became 'Holiness unto the Lord'.

It may be, of course, that the touching of the Sin Offering refers primarily to the offerer, who, when he brought his offering pressed his hands upon it and thus identified himself with it in a ceremonial way. And this may be an illustration of what happens when a sinner trusts the Saviour.

> *My faith would lay its hand,*
> *On that dear head of Thine;*
> *While like a penitent I stand,*
> *And there confess my sin.*

The laying on of the offerer's hands was also a feature of the burnt offering. There, as we have pointed out, this act symbolised the ceremonial transference or imputation of the merit and value of the offering to the offerer. But in the case of the Sin

Offering, although the act was the same, the meaning is different. Here the laying on of hands signified the transference or imputation of the offerer's sins to his sacrifice. And so in these two offerings we have illustrated the two sides to the truth of imputation. The outworking of this imputed righteousness of God will be seen in a daily manner of life that is righteous.

From the precise moment of our faith in the Lord Jesus we are, 'Holiness unto the Lord'. And the holiness of God, expressed in our manner of living, is the strongest proof that we really are the Lord's. We often sing, "There's power in the blood"; but what does such language mean? The Sin Offering supplies the answer. We believe that there is such inherent power in Jesus blood, that when we identify ourselves with Him by faith, we are instantly transformed from being 'sinners in our sins' to being 'Holiness unto the Lord'.

The complete manifestation of this must, admittedly, await the coming of the Lord, but in the meantime, progressive sanctification means that the believer is always reaching after a greater measure of holiness in his life. Sanctification has been well defined as the bringing of our *state* (what we are before men) into line with our *standing* (what we are before God). The oft repeated exhortation to Israel to 'Sanctify themselves' has equal force for us.

The need for reverence

A rather strange and somewhat severe instruction was given about the blood of the Sin Offering. "When there is sprinkled of the blood upon any garment, thou shalt wash that whereon it was sprinkled in the Holy Place. But the earthen vessel wherein it is [boiled] shall be broken; and if it be [boiled] in a [bronze] pot, it shall be both scoured, and rinsed in water". (Lev.6:27,28) It may be that this instruction had in view a possible accident. Even so, it is remarkable that in the event of some of the blood falling on a garment, such detailed instructions were given about how the garment was to be handled.

It was to be (i) washed, (ii) and then boiled, (iii) in the Holy Place, (iv) the earthen vessel was to be broken, never to be used again, and (v) if the vessel was of bronze it was to be both scoured and rinsed in water. Such processes were enjoined upon the people in order to instil into them a due reverence for the blood. And we must never forget that the blood of those sacrifices pointed forward in a dramatic way, to the blood of Christ, which, as scripture constantly reminds us, is precious beyond price.

Holiness and reverence

And so we have two things here which go hand in hand. A true appreciation of Holiness and a due reverence for Divine things. The Psalmist linked these two things when he said, "Holy and reverend is His name." (Psa.111:9) As the curtain falls on the twentieth century, one of its most marked features is that nothing is sacred any more. Secularism and materialism have removed from us a sense of the reverence that earlier generations believed was due to the Almighty. Solomon called it 'the fear of the Lord' and insisted that it is the beginning of wisdom. The consequences, a rising tide of crime and moral turpitude, are already appalling and the end is not yet. (Matt.24:6)

The immediate reason for this loss is that we no longer have a true estimate of God's Holiness. In fact, we scarcely take into our reckoning, that "God is a consuming fire." Yet when Moses and the children of Israel crossed the Red Sea they sung this song unto the Lord, "...Who is like unto thee, O Lord, among the gods? Who is like unto thee, glorious in holiness, fearful in praises, doing wonders?" Since holiness is the very excellence of the Divine nature, only a recovery of a sense of the holiness of God will restore to us a due and becoming spirit of reverence.

One final word. Accepting the limitations implicit in those constantly repeated sacrifices, what assurance did they minister to the Israelites who offered them? How could they be sure that the particular sin for which they had brought them really was forgiven? Their assurance rested upon what God had said about those sacrifices. His word declared, "It shall be forgiven." (See Lev.4:20,26,31,35.) Israel's assurance on the passover night in Egypt also rested upon these two things, the blood of the Lamb and the word of the Lord. And to-day, we who rejoice in Christ and who rest by faith upon the witness of God's word, find here our blessed assurance too.

the tresspass offering

(Scripture Leviticus 5:1-6:7, 7:1-10.)

N.T. Fulfilment - "Christ died for our sins aacording to the scriptures; He was delivered for our offences, and raised again for our justification." (1Cor.15:3. Rom.4:25)

AS ALREADY STATED, THE SIN AND TRESPASS OFFERINGS DIFFERED FROM THE OTHER THREE OFFERINGS IN THAT THEY WERE NOT SAID TO BE SWEET SAVOUR OFFERINGS. This was because they were offerings for sin and because God demanded a Sin Offering and a Trespass Offering. The other offerings were all voluntary. But there is nothing voluntary where sin is concerned. And as for our conduct, we are solemnly forewarned that every one of us must give account of himself to God.

We have also noted that distinguishing between these two offerings is not easy. In broad terms the Sin Offering deals with the person of the sinner whereas the Trespass Offering deals with the sins he has committed. But because of their very nature there must inevitably be some overlapping. Some see the instructions for the Sin Offering running right through from Ch.4 to Ch.5v13 but this is just an indication of the overlapping we have referred to. We shall follow the chapter division and begin our study of the Trespass Offering at Ch.5v1.

The Sin Offering has in view the need for the sinner to be judicially cleared of the guilt of his sin, but the Trespass Offering is concerned about the effect that his sin has had in every de partment of his life. The Trespass Offering may be said to view sin in two different and quite distinct ways. First, as a defilement needing to be purged, and then as a debt needing to be paid. Both ideas will be familiar to us and especially the second for we are often confronted with a notice reading, "Trespassers will be prosecuted."

Defilement

As believers in the Lord Jesus Christ we are strangers and pilgrims in the earth. We are passing through a defiling world, and the chapter before us identifies several channels through which we can become defiled. For instance, "If a soul sin, and hear..." (Lev.5:1) We are defiled by the things we hear. Times without number we have been able to identify with righteous Lot who was vexed by the filthy conversation of Sodom. We must not neglect to set a regular watch over against eargate.

Again, "If a soul touch any unclean thing..." (Lev.5:2,3) There are many things that Christians ought not even to touch. And yet in spite of ourselves there is the inevitable contact with defiling influences. "If a soul make an oath pronouncing with his lips..." (Lev.5:4) Sometimes our speech is an offence both to God and man, and we are thereby defiled.

We might add that we can easily be defiled by what we see. It was carelessness at this point that led David into his great sin with Bathsheba. The consequences of that sin were both unforeseen and very far reaching. David's family was profoundly affected by his failure as was his kingdom and his throne. But beyond all that, we learn in his great penitential psalm, that David eventually came to see, that his sin was primarily against God. (Psa.51:4)

There are many other channels through which we may become defiled. We should constantly guard against sin in our conduct and we must be especially on our guard lest we should ever foolishly consider ourselves immune to sin's defiling influence. A timely admonishment in the presence of temptation in any form is, "Let him who thinks he stands take heed lest he fall." (1Cor.10:12)

In the event of someone becoming defiled, what should be done about it? Let the record speak. "It shall be, when he shall be guilty in one of these things, that he shall *confess* that he has sinned *in that thing*." (Lev.5:5) Sin is like leprosy, it is never said to be healed, it is always cleansed; and there are two cleansings from sin alluded to in the scriptures.

There is an initial cleansing when we are converted. "The blood of Jesus Christ, God's Son, cleanseth us from all sin." (1John 1:7) This is a legal or judicial clearing of the sinner from the guilt of his sins, accomplished in virtue of Jesus blood. It is the Sin Offering aspect of forgiveness. But then there is a practical cleansing from the defilement of sin. "If we confess our sins, He is faithful and just to forgive us our sins and to cleanse us from all unrighteousness." (1John 1:9)

The first of these cleansings is conditioned on our *believing* and it is a *once for all* cleansing. "To Him [i.e. Jesus] give all the prophets witness, that through His name whosoever believes in Him shall receive remission of sins." (Acts 10:43) A sinner in his sins must be pointed to Christ and urged to believe in Him as the gaoler at Phillipi was urged to do. Paul said, "Believe on the Lord Jesus Christ and you will be saved." (Acts 16:31)

But oftentimes believers themselves become defiled and stand in need of cleansing. In the very nature of things, this cleansing is not a once for all experience. On the contrary, it needs to be constantly repeated. Now forgiveness for believers is always conditioned on *confessing*. "He shall *confess* that he has sinned *in that thing*." (Lev.5:5) The significance of this should be carefully noted.

Three factors enter into true confession. In the first place, there must be a recognition of that specific sin for what it really is. We must call a spade, a spade. And here the scriptures are very specific, "He shall confess that he has sinned *in that thing*." Then, secondly, we must turn from it; this is where repentance comes in. Take a concordance and note how often scripture links forgiveness with repentance. Finally we must claim the Lord's promise and rest upon His word, "if we confess our sins, He is faithful and just to forgive us our sins." (1John 1:9)

The many Sacrifices - the one Sacrifice

But there was something else the trespasser had to do. "He shall bring his Trespass Offering unto the Lord for his sin... and the priest shall make an atonement for him for his sin... and it shall be forgiven him." (Lev.5:6-10) Those Old Testament sacrifices served to cover over sins until Christ. But that is all they did. It was when He came and went to the cross, that all the accumulated of sin which had been covered over, was taken up and laid on Him.

And then at the same time God anticipated all the sins of these last days, and at the cross He made to meet, and to rest, upon the Lord Jesus the sum total of human sin. He became "the satisfaction for our sins, and not for ours only, but also for the sins of the whole world." (See 1John 2:2.) The Trespass Offering speaks most profoundly of Christ who was "delivered for our offences."

At the precise time when Jesus died, all our individual sins were still future. This means that God has dealt judicially and in advance, with all the sins we have ever committed or may yet commit. All our open sins and all our secret sins were laid on

Jesus; those sins which, if they were projected on to a screen in some public place, would cause us to blush with shame, and to hide ourselves, and never show ourselves again in public. God, who knew them, laid them on Jesus when He died for our sins according to the scriptures.

And so when believers sin, the forgiveness of God, which is conditioned upon confession, may be experienced on the basis of an atonement already made. In dealing with sin, God must always act in a way consistent with His own righteous character. The Trespass Offering teaches the ground upon which God is able to forgive our sins, without compromising His own right-eousness. A sinner pleading the sacrifice of Christ for his sins to-day is the antitype of an Israelite bringing a Trespass Offering in that day. There is forgiveness with God that He may be feared, a forgiveness purchased at infinite cost. It necessitated the shed-ding of the precious blood of God's beloved Son.

The trespass offering may have taken any one of three forms.

(1) Lambs or kids

It may have been a lamb or a kid from the flocks. In that event, the animal chosen was to be the female of the species. The fact that a female was chosen must surely have some meaning and we must pause to consider what that meaning might be. Wherever the Christian gospel has prevailed, the role and status of womanhood has always been elevated. This can be confirmed by a quiet word with any overseas missionary. But throughout the western world, there are ominous signs that this process is going into reverse. And this in spite of, or perhaps even because of, the activities of the many feminist agencies that have mush-roomed in recent years. Its attitude to the dignity and integrity of womanhood and motherhood is a touchstone of any society.

The Christian position on this issue is clearly stated in Peter's epistle, "husbands give honour unto the wife, as unto the weaker vessel." (1Pet.3:7) Because the wife is the weaker vessel, added honour is bestowed upon her. In the light of Peter's statement it seems quite clear that the lamb or kid of the Trespass Offering, being a female, speaks of the Lord Jesus appearing in this world in human weakness. We tend to dwell on the Saviour's power; and we have glimpses of that during His ministry, especially in His miracles, but His power became really manifest only in His resurrection from the dead.

Crucified in weakness

During His life on earth our Lord voluntarily subjected Himself to every sinless weakness known to us. When He sat by the side of Jacob's well, it was because He was weary with the journey. We know, of course, that the everlasting God fainteth not, neither is weary; but in manhood Jesus was conscious of physical weariness. He also knew the pangs of hunger and of thirst.

And He voluntarily subjected Himself to His foes, who could have had no power at all except it were given them from above. He gave His back to the smiters and His cheeks to them that plucked off the hair. In the Judgement hall, He could have called ten thousand angels, but He uttered not a word. And finally, He subjected Himself to all the indignities of the cross, saying, "Father, not my will but thine be done." Truly, when He humbled Himself our Saviour assumed the place of complete subjection to the Father's will.

(2) Doves or pigeons

But perhaps the offerer could not afford a lamb or a kid. In that event, he might bring a couple of turtle doves or two young pigeons. (Lev.5:7) These two birds combined to set forth the two aspects of the Trespass Offering. One became a Sin Offering, teaching us that the death of the cross was because of our sins, "He was delivered for our offences." (Rom.4:24) The other bird became a Burnt Offering, which, as we have already shown, has in view the Godward side of things rather than what is man ward.

In His death for our sins, the Lord Jesus met every claim of divine holiness. And having so satisfied God, Paul was able to write, "God was in Christ reconciling the world unto Himself, not imputing their trespasses unto them, and has committed to us the word of reconciliation." (2Cor.5:19) Because of Calvary there can now be both a non-imputation of sin, and an imputation of righteousness, to all who believe in Jesus. (See Rom.4:6-8.)

"The word is near you" said Paul, and the Trespass Offering bears witness to how near forgiveness has been brought to man. The living God took account of every possible human weakness so that if a person could not bring a lamb or a kid or even an offering of two pigeons, provision was made for the Trespass Offering to take the form of "the tenth part of an ephah of fine flour." (Lev.5:11) Forgiveness was within the reach of all. In this aspect of the Trespass Offering there was no blood shedding but still it speaks of Christ.

(3) Fine Flour

The tenth part of an ephah takes us back to the giving of the manna. (See Ex.16.) That the manna coming down from heaven speaks of our Lord in His self-humbling does not need to be argued. But it will be remembered how Moses instructed Aaron to take an omer of the manna, as a memorial, and put it into a golden pot. This was then deposited in the Ark of the covenant, which, in turn, was kept in the Most Holy Place after the Tabernacle was constructed. With even an elementary knowledge of the significance of the Tabernacle in the wilderness, we should have no difficulty in seeing in that memorial omer in the Most Holy Place, a foreshadowing of Christ risen, exalted and glorified in the presence of God.

But what is the connection between all this, and the Trespass Offering? Well, the final verse of the chapter on the manna says, "Now an omer is the tenth part of an ephah." (Ex.16:36) The tenth part of an ephah of fine flour as a Trespass Offering may represent a very feeble appre-hension of Christ, but it is enough. It is not the greatness or otherwise of our faith that matters, but the greatness of Him in whom our faith reposes.

Taken together the three forms of the Trespass Offering present a marvellously comprehensive view of our Saviour. They trace a line through His life and ministry on earth, and through the sorrows and sufferings of His death, to His resurrection and His Ascension. They pursue His course right up to the throne of God. How impoverished we would be if we did not have the record of these Levitical Offerings which cast such a wonderful light upon our way.

But the Trespass Offering also views sin as a debt needing to be paid. "If a soul commit a trespass, and sin through ignorance in the holy things of the Lord." (v.15) In the next chapter, the trespass committed is against another person, but here it is specifically against the Lord. Of course, all sin is ulti-mately against God. We have already mentioned David's peni-tential Psalm in which he expresses his deep exercise of heart after the affair with Bathsheba. The wrong he had done was against both Bathsheba and Uriah, but in this Psalm he cries out, "Against thee, thee only, have I sinned, and done this evil in thy sight." (Psa 51:4)

Things sacred

In our day 'The holy things of the Lord' are largely cast aside. They are treated as common. Nevertheless, they are precious to the Lord and He will not hold guiltless the person who lightly esteems them. In the last paragraph of the book of Leviticus the holy things of the Lord are represented in terms of tithes and offerings. At first this may seem strange, until one remembers that there never was blessing in Israel when the tithes and offerings were neglected. Hence the important call of Malachi, "Bring all the tithes into the storehouse, and prove me now, says the Lord of Hosts, if I will not open for you the windows of heaven,and pour out for you a blessing, that there shall not be room enough to receive it." (Mal.3:10)

At this point, the discussion of the Trespass Offering assumes the case of a farmer who underestimated his crops. In consequence he brought to the treasury of the Lord's house an impoverished tithe. When the error was discovered, his duty was to bring a Trespass Offering to make an atonement for the wrong he had done. And then, in addition to that, he was required to make amends for that wrong. This was done by bringing, along with his Trespass Offering, the amount of the shortfall and also by adding to it an additional fifth part. The result was that when all was settled, the treasury of the Lord's house was advantaged by whatever may have been the amount of the fifth part of the shortfall.

That there is a practical lesson in all this for us, hardly needs to be argued. The question was asked in olden time, "Will a man rob God? Yet you have robbed me. But you say, How have we robbed God? In tithes and offerings." (Mal.3:8) One of Solomon's proverbs says, "Honour the Lord with your substance, and with the firstfruits of all your increase; so shall your barns be filled with plenty, and your presses shall burst out with new wine." (Prov.3:9,10) Failure at this point has robbed God of His due and has robbed the church of much blessing.

The Fullness of Redemption

But it is the typical meaning of the Trespass Offering and the making of amends that we wish to consider. When the Lord Jesus offered Himself without spot to God, He died for our trespasses, and thus He became our great Trespass Offering. But we must not think that when He paid the price of sin, He merely paid the bare minimum to unlock the gate of heaven and let us in. Just enough to allow us to scrape through. The reality is that He paid into the bank of heaven a ransom, the value of which is far more than sufficient to pay for all the sins of every penitent sinner.

That God can make even the wrath of man to praise Him, was supremely demonstrated at Calvary. For the Lord Jesus not only paid the price of sin, He went further, He made amends and added the fifth part thereto, so that God has actually brought blessing out of cursing. Paul carries us back to Calvary, to the place where sin abounded, and he shows us that right there in that very place "grace did *much more* abound." (Rom.5:20)

> *"In Him the tribes of Adam gain,*
> *More blessings, than their father lost."*

God too has gained through redemption. Man's sin robbed God of His glory. But in His death Jesus could say, "Then I restored that which I took not away." (Psa.69:4) A point of great significance was reached when our Saviour cried out, in anguish of spirit, "Now is my soul troubled; and what shall I say? [this is what I shall say] Father, glorify thy name. Then there came a voice from heaven, saying, I have both glorified it, and will glorify it again." (John 12:27,28) A fifth part is a double tenth or tithe, and it may be that it points to how the Lord Jesus glorified God's name in this double sense, first, by His life, (*I have glorified it*) and then, by His death (*I will glorify it again*).

The immediate significance for us of the double tithe or fifth part may be illustrated from the life of Joseph. After the famine in Egypt from which the people had only found deliverance through Joseph, it became an ordinance that the fifth part of their annual increase was paid to Pharaoh. The land and the people had belonged to Pharaoh before the famine, but now as a result of Joseph's work, Pharaoh had a further claim upon the people, and upon all that belonged to them. It was an additional claim that he did not have before. (See Gen.47:18-26.)

Restitution

Since God is the creator of all, He has a creatorial claim upon all. But now, on the ground of redemption, He has a wholly new claim upon His own. The only worthy response we can make to that claim is to "Present our bodies a living sacrifice, holy, and acceptable unto God, which is our reasonable service." (Rom.12:1) Thereafter, everything we do or give, in the service of God, is simply a token of the fact that we are the Lord's. Just as the Egyptians gave the double tithe or the fifth part as a token that they now belonged to Pharaoh in an altogether new and special sense.

Leviticus chapter six highlights the manward side of the Trespass Offering. While all sin is primarily against God, sometimes a third party may be injured by our offence. A neighbour may have put us on trust in some matter, and we might have broken that trust. Or it may be a matter of fellowship (*margin; a bargain*), and we have not kept our side of the bargain. (Lev.6:2) Perhaps we have been guilty of a blatant theft; we may even have found something that a neighbour had lost and we have knowingly concealed it from him. If in any or all of these things we are guilty, what are we to do?

The Israelite of old would have had recourse to the Trespass Offering and through it he would have found the forgiveness of God. But first, he was obliged to make restitution to the neighbour who had been wronged. "He shall restore that which he took violently away, etc." (Lev.6:4) As well as that, he was required to add a fifth part to the amount, the valuation being measured by the standards of the house of God.

The principle of restitution was firmly established in the Old Testament and, to this day, it has never been abrogated. It was maintained by Paul in his epistle to Philemon. A runaway slave called Onesimus had defrauded his believing master; and now, in the meantime, he had been converted. In pleading his cause, Paul did not ignore what Onesimus had done. He openly acknowledged it, and promised on his behalf, to make restitution to Philemon. (See the epistle to Philemon.)

But perhaps the best known instance of this principle is the case of Zacchaeus, the tax-collector who received Christ at Jericho. "Lord, he said, the half of my goods I give to the poor; and if I have taken anything from any man by false accusation, I restore him fourfold." (Luke19:8) Restitution is never advocated as a condition of salvation, but it is a very definite evidence that a true work of grace has been done in the heart.

It is not difficult to imagine the impact upon an unconverted person, when one who has recently come to Christ is willing to make amends for some offence committed in the past. Alas, the subject is seldom mentioned in gospel circles to-day, and to that extent the effectiveness of the testimony has become diluted. At the same time it needs to be said, that when this question is raised, it calls for very wise and careful handling. Nevertheless, the principle of restitution stands and the enjoyment of God's forgiveness requires that it be honoured.

It is most holy

In conclusion, we must call attention to a very important detail. Four times in the law of the Sin Offering and in the law of the Trespass Offering we read, "It is most holy." (Lev.6:25,29 & 7:1,6) The scriptures go to great lengths to emphasise the personal sinlessness of the Lord Jesus even at the very time when He became our sin-bearer. Although our sins were laid on Him, He was personally sinless. "He knew no sin" (2Cor.5:21), and "He did no sin" (1Pet.2:22). We must stress that when God laid on Him the iniquity of us all, even at that point, the truth of His personal impeccability remained inviolate. It was still true, "in Him is no sin." (1John 3:5)

The only other offering to be designated 'most holy' was the Meal Offering. (Lev.6:17) Speaking as it does of the perfect life of Christ, it combines with the Sin and Trespass Offerings to underscore the unique sinlessness of our Saviour both in His life and in His death. Despite repeated attempts by His enemies to impute evil to His name, either by claiming that His miracles were wrought by the power of Beelzebub (Matt.12:24), or by falsely accusing Him of blasphemy because He claimed to be the Son of God (Matt.26:65), the Holy Spirit maintains in the scriptures an uncompromising testimony to His absolute sinlessness.

The actual day of His death was the day that also witnessed the most concentrated testimony to His innocence. At its beginning, Pilate's wife wrote to her husband, "Have nothing to do with that just man." And then at its close the centurion, overwhelmed by what he had seen, was heard to say, "Certainly this was a righteous man." While in the intervening hours, at the one extreme Pilate admitted, "I find no fault in Him." and at the other, the dying thief exclaimed, "This man has done nothing amiss." Thus, no room is left for the slightest doubt about the person of our Saviour. Made sin for us, He was personally unsullied and unspotted.

> *Because the sinless Saviour died,*
> *My sinful soul is counted free;*
> *For God, the just, is satisfied,*
> *To look on Him and pardon me.*

epilogue

IT HAS BEEN SAID THAT COMING EVENTS CAST THEIR SHADOWS BEFORE THEM. THIS WAS CERTAINLY TRUE OF CALVARY'S CROSS. ITS HISTORY REACHES BACK INTO eternity and it's shadows have been upon the human story since the garden of Eden. The sacrifice that provided a covering for the nakedness of our first parents pointed forward to the cross, as did the ministrations of Abel at the gates of Eden.

With the passage of time the shadows became more clearly defined, until Abraham's faith received its severest test. "Take now your son, your only son, whom you love so dearly, and offer him in the place that I will show you." (Gen.22:1,2) In the record of that ancient sacrifice, we are able to read in lines, both clear and plain, the meaning of what must be the tenderest statement in the New Testament, "God spared not His own Son." The twenty second and the sixty ninth Psalms and the fifty third chapter of Isaiah, along with a host of other scriptures, combine to bring us ultimately to stand with unshod feet before the Saviour's cross.

When we turn to the five principle offerings of the Levitical system, we find ourselves again treading the Calvary Road. It is inconceivable that one who claims to love the Lord could be indifferent to such unfoldings of the secrets of the heart of God, as are laid before us in those various offerings. Their teaching permeates the total revelation God has given to us in the sacred scriptures.

The first thing that exercises the awakened sinner is the question of his sins. The eternal remedy is found in the person and work of the Crucified, who was wounded for our transgressions and bruised for our iniquities. This is the message of the Trespass Offering. But what about the sinner himself? The Sin Offering teaches us that believing sinners are justified before God in virtue of Jesus' blood: they are given a perfect standing before the throne of God.

But stripping the sinner of his sins and justifying him from all things is not the end of the story, it is just the beginning. The Peace Offering assures us that the saved sinner is also brought into a completely new position where he is able to enjoy peace with God. He is now able to participate in a new fellowship, with the Father and with His Son, and with all who call upon the Name of our Lord Jesus Christ.

To leave the matter there would be wonderful indeed, but the Meal Offering reminds us that all this is only possible because of the laying down in death of a perfect life. The living of that life did not save us, but it demonstrated its suitability to be laid down, as a sacrifice for sins, to make atonement for our souls.

And then the Burnt Offering, which was burnt wholly to ashes on the altar of sacrifice, highlights the supreme aspect of the cross. It tells of God's satisfaction with the work of His Son and impresses upon our minds, that the issue above all other issues, is not what we think of ourselves, but what God thinks of Christ. And so from a subjective preoccupation with ourselves and our sins, the offerings bring us into the heavenly places where our preoccupation is with Christ in glory and our standing and position in Him.

The study of the offerings has exercised many minds across the years. It is unlikely that any who have written or spoken on this theme have been completely satisfied with their work. There are so many permutations to the offerings, as there are so many facets and aspects to the cross; one feels like a child paddling along the shore of a great ocean. But then eternal days will be far too short to exhaust the truly amazing theme of these remarkable scriptures. Should the reader have found some profit in reading these pages, may he make the author's desire his own, to cry with his latest breath, "Behold the Lamb."

appendice one
The Continual Burnt Offering
(Exodus 29:38-46)

THE OFFERINGS WE HAVE CONSIDERED WERE USED BY THE PEOPLE, NOT ONLY INDIVIDUALLY BUT ALSO NATIONALLY. SOME OF THE SACRIFICES WERE OFFERED FOR THE NATION on an annual basis as, for instance, on the great day of atonement. (See Lev.16.) But there was one sacrifice that was persented daily for the whole nation.

It was an ordinance in Israel that every day two lambs were selected for sacrifice. One lamb was slain in the morning and offered on the altar of burnt offering, and then the same exercise was repeated with the second lamb in the evening. This was known as the morning and the evening sacrifice. It was a daily routine, and because of its repetitive nature it was also called the continual Burnt Offering.

This was clearly a most significant sacrifice. Our Lord was crucified at the time of the morning sacrifice and He died at the time of the evening sacrifice. And since the Burnt Offering was the offering of consecration, it was a twice daily reminder to the people that they belonged to the Lord. Moreover, in maintaining this ordinance the people were ceremoniously placed under the protection of the slain lamb, both at the beginning and at the end of each day.

Realising His presence

But there was another side to the continual Burnt Offering. It was on the basis of this sacrifice that the Lord had said He would *meet* with His people and *speak* to them. (v.42,43) On this ground He would *dwell* among them, and He would also so reveal Himself to them, that they would know that He was the Lord their God, who brought them forth out of the land of Egypt. (v.45,46) And so the realisation of these privileges was made dependant on their faithfulness in maintaining the morning and evening sacrifice.

In the first chapter of Genesis we are told that "the evening and the morning were the first day" etc. Evidently the living God took the work of creation on a day by day basis, and this must say something to us. David, the sweet Psalmist of Israel, was committed to the idea of a regular daily routine of spiritual exercise, for he said, "It is a good thing...to show forth thy lovingkindness in the morning, and thy faithfulness every night." (Psa. 92:1,2) By the brook Cherith, every morning and every evening, the ravens brought food to Elijah; and every day Daniel maintained an open window towards Jerusalem. He prayed daily to His God, every morning, noon and night. We too, need a daily spiritual routine.

Dr. Barnhouse began his commentary on the book of *Genesis* with this observation, "If our day does not start with the Lord, there can be no blessing. If it does start with Him, there can be nothing but blessing." The continual Burnt Offering teaches us, therefore, the importance of regular spiritual exercise, on a daily basis, before the Lord. We must begin each day aright, if we are to enjoy a sense of His presence with us in the onward march of life. And then at its close we should not withhold our sacrifice of thanksgiving for the goodness and mercy that has followed us throughout another day.

The Presence in three senses

The Lord's presence is brought before us in at least three senses in scripture. First, there is His presence in its universal sense, for He is omnipresent. In this sense, whether we realise it or not, all of us, all of the time, are in His presence. (See Psa.139:7-12.) But we also speak of the secret of His presence, when we retire from the rush and bustle of life, and draw near to Him to seek His face in prayer. And finally there is the realised and enjoyed presence of the Lord with His people. Two people might be in the same house and one not realise that the other is present; two people might be in the same room, and neither may be enjoying the other's presence.

He has said, "My presence shall go with you" (Ex.33:14) and "I will never leave you, nor forsake you." (Hebs.13:5) and "Lo, I am with you always." (Matt.28:20) To know the Lord's presence with us, is to prove His grace and power in the varied circumstances of daily living. But the realisation of these promises and the conscious enjoyment of His presence calls for those spiritual conditions in us, that are foreshadowed in the continual Burnt Offering.

And then, in the context of home and family life, Christian parents should not neglect to place themselves and their families every morning under the protection of the slain lamb. And as the shadows lengthen and the darkness closes in, that exercise should be repeated every night. We do not have an altar of brass, but every Christian home should have a Family Altar. Whatever we choose to call it, the morning and evening sacrifice should be maintained by us all whatever the cost.

appendice two
Keeping the fire burning
(Lev. 6:8-13)

IN OUR OPENING CHAPTER WE ESTABLISHED THAT THE
BURNT OFFERING WAS THE OFFERING OF CONSECRATION.
IT SIGNIFIES DEVOTION TO THE LORD; BOTH CHRIST'S
devotion and ours. The difficulty with devotion is that it tends to
wax and wane, it can so easily grow cold. This is recognised even in
our type, for a solemn charge was laid upon the people to keep the
fire burning on the altar of burnt offering. "It is the burnt altar, because of the burning all night unto the morning, the fire of the altar
shall be burning in it." (v.9) "The fire on the altar shall not be put
out. It shall ever be burning, it shall never be put out." (v. 12,13)

Burning low

When Samuel was still a boy in the temple at Shiloh he
noticed that the lamp was burning dim. This was just a reflection of
the spiritual condition of the people of God at that time. Later,
through the prophet Jeremiah, the Lord lamented the state of back-
sliding Israel. He said, "I remember you, the kindness ... the love ...
when you went after me in the wilderness. Israel was holiness unto
the Lord, and the firstfruits of his increase." (Jer. 2:2,3) But now all
was only just a memory.

The Christians at Ephesus too, had left their first love, while
those at Laodicea had allowed themselves to become lukewarm. (See
Rev:2&3.) And too often, we ourselves are like Simon Peter when he

walked afar off. If the fire of devotion has not gone out completely, it is certainly not aflame.

> *Where is the blessedness I knew,*
> *When first I saw the Lord;*
> *Where is the soul refreshing view,*
> *O Jesus and His word.*
> *What peaceful hours I once enjoyed,*
> *How sweet their memory still;*
> *But they have left an aching void,*
> *This world can never fill.*

Keeping the fire burning on the altar was primarily a duty of the priests. And since we are believer-priests, it is not difficult to see in this a matter of individual responsibility. Whatever other charges we may bear, our first duty is always the maintenance of our own personal relationship with the Lord. We should never have to confess, "They made me a keeper of vineyards, but my own vineyard have I not kept." (S.o.S.1:6) We must "Keep the heart with all diligence, for out of it are the issues of life". (Prov. 4:23) So said the wise man and his advice is as relevant as it is timeless.

Removing the Ashes

To keep the fire on the altar burning, it was necessary for the ashes to be removed at regular intervals. In carrying out this task the priest had to put on his linen garments, take up the ashes, and lay them beside the altar. He then laid aside those garments and put on other garments, in order to carry the ashes outside the camp to a clean place. This repeated changing of his clothes is, to our way of thinking, a rather puzzling requirement.

Whatever other significance may be read into this exercise, we know that the old Anglo-saxon word for clothes is **habits**. And we know that the language of the English Bible has its roots in the anglo-saxon. Keeping this in mind can help us to understand, what otherwise, might be meaningless. We know how vitally important it is to maintain healthy habits in the Christian life. The important thing about this change of clothing on the part of the priest was that it was not optional, it was a divine requirement, it was the word of the Lord. The lesson for us must be that an attitude of subjection to that word is just as vital to a believer-priest to-day as it was to the sons of Aaron all those many years ago.

The charge is sometimes made that people may attend the Lord's table simply out of habit. While this must be better than the habit, commonly indulged, of simply ignoring this precious ordinance, such a charge stands or falls on the spiritual condition of the person who attends. The word of God and prayer are the two legs on which the Christian stands. We must apply ourselves intelligently to them, both in private and in the fellowship of the church. To absent ourselves unnecessarily from the place of corporate Bible study and prayer is probably the first sign that the lamp is burning dim and the fires of devotion are beginning to wane.

Replenshing the Wood

As well as the removal of the ashes there was also the replenishing of the wood. "The priest shall burn wood on it every morning." (v.12) The wood obviously speaks of future fires just as the ashes speak of former fires. Taken together, these two exercises may point us to Paul's resolve, "forgetting those things that are behind, and reaching forth unto those things that are before, I press toward the mark for the prize of the high calling of God in Christ Jesus." (See Phil.3:13,14.) The temptation to bask in the afterglow of the fires of former successes can only spell disaster in the Christian life.

The law of the burnt offering then, has a very practical message for us. It enjoins upon us, as a matter of vital importance, the need to maintain our devotion to the Lord on a daily basis. Whatever the past may hold, of failure or success, we dare not allow it to stand in our way, as we press towards the goal for the prize. We must, at all costs, keep the fires of devotion burning on 'the mean altar of the heart'. Others may do as they please, "but as for me and my house, we will serve the Lord." (Josh. 24:15)